thinking
smart
you are how you think

thinking
smart
you are how you think

applying the **theory of constraints**
in developing **thinking skills**

KHAW CHOON EAN

Pelanduk
Publications

Published by
Pelanduk Publications (M) Sdn Bhd
(Co. No. 113307-W)
12 Jalan SS13/3E
Subang Jaya Industrial Estate
47500 Subang Jaya
Selangor Darul Ehsan, Malaysia.

Address all correspondence to
Pelanduk Publications (M) Sdn Bhd
P.O. Box 8265, 46785 Kelana Jaya
Selangor Darul Ehsan, Malaysia.
Website: *www.pelanduk.com*
e-mail: *rusaone@tm.net.my*

Perpustakaan Negara Malaysia   Cataloguing-in-Publication Data
     Think smart: you are how you think: applying the theory of
     constraints in developing thinking skills/by Khaw Choon Ean
     Includes index
     ISBN 967-978-918-7
     1. Thought and thinking. 2. Creative thinking. 3. Critical thinking.
     I. Title.
     153.42

Printed and bound in Malaysia.

Contents

Foreword
Preface
Acknowledgements
Introduction
About the Author

Foreword

Thinking skills for the solution of problems and conflicts is a topic near to my heart. In 1999, I was the only Malaysian presenter at the 8th International Conference on Thinking in Edmonton, Canada during which I had the opportunity of attending a presentation by Kishore Mahbubani, who asked the very provocative question "Can Asians Think?"

This led me to ask the question "Can Malaysians Think Well? The answer to this question is not easy, because this involves various factors including world view and mindset of the Malaysian nation and on the whole, one cannot answer a definite yes or no to the question.

To answer a definite yes, the nation's mindset needs to be changed and this involves making quantum leaps in the education of the entire population of the nation. It is not an easy task because it means a great deal of hard work, perseverance and taking the challenge in the first place.

I decided to take the first steps of this challenge with the help of Khaw Choon Ean, after all WHO WOULD NOT WANT TO USE THINKING SKILLS IN ONE'S DAILY ACTIVITIES? It was with this goal in mind that *"Thinking Smart: You Are How You Think — Applying the Theory of Constraints in Developing Thinking Skills"* was born.

I first learnt about the Theory of Constraints for Education (TOCFE) at the 8th International Conference on Thinking in Edmonton, Canada as I mentioned earlier. I saw its strength immediately and started working with the CEO and President of TOCFE, Inc., Kathy Suerken, on how to introduce it into Malaysia.

I decided to share my discovery with the Curriculum Development Centre of the Malaysian Ministry of Education. It was here that I was fortunate to meet Khaw Choon Ean, who was the Head of Special Projects and her Director who at that time was Dr. Sharifah Maimunah Syed Zin. There was an immediate desire to take up these thinking tools and the rest is history.

Khaw Choon Ean and I were fortunate that TOCFE, Inc offered to train us if we were willing to devote our time and to commit ourselves for its introduction into Malaysia. Thus in 2001 we were part of an international team to undergo an intensive course in Monterrey, Mexico.

We left Mexico with a mission, that is, to ensure that the Theory of Constraints was introduced into Malaysia for the sake of our future generation of children and the nation's prosperity as a whole. Since then TOCFE has made great inroads in Malaysian schools and soon we hope to have it introduced into universities.

I would like to congratulate Khaw Choon Ean on her efforts to produce *"Thinking Smart: You Are How You Think — Applying the Theory of Constraints in Developing Thinking Skills"* as a book. It marks the beginning of an introduction to thinking tools that even kindergarten children can use. It is also a commitment to sharing with society at large, ways of developing a thinking nation which is a necessity in this era of globalization.

Malaysian school children are fortunate that the Theory of Constraints is now incorporated into the school curriculum. Thus, the publication of this book by Ean, as I fondly call her, is timely in that parents can now begin to reinforce not only their children's thinking skills but also their own. It is something that both parents and children can work at together leading to harmony within the family unit.

As you read *"Thinking Smart: You Are How You Think —
Applying the Theory of Constraints in Developing Thinking Skills"*
you may be challenged to rethink the way you have been managing
not only your own problems but also that of your children. You
will probably be excited by the possibility of gains in resolving
problems easily – that you usually used to dream about.

Khaw Choon Ean has organized the tried-out materials in an
easy, exciting and motivating way and children, parents and
teachers, in fact, anyone, will find the manner in which the materials
are presented simple to follow as well as thought provoking and
generating other ideas.

TOC thinking tools have helped me solved countless problems
professionally and domestically. In short, it has made a difference
in my life and I know that it will help many others too. This is a
powerful yet flexible set of thinking tools which can lead to quality
communication to convince yourself or another person to change
for improvement.

*"Thinking Smart: You Are How You Think — Applying the
Theory of Constraints in Developing Thinking Skills"* promises to
influence education and society at large far into the future.

'A journey of a thousand miles, begins with a single step'
— ANCIENT CHINESE PROVERB.

Assoc. Prof. Dr. Shameem Rafik-Galea
Universiti Putra Malaysia

The Theory of Constraints develops your ability to solve problems and make responsible and effective decisions with commitment. Effective and responsible thinking skills as well as clear communication of thinking are developed.

These tools are applicable to thinking about behaviour leading to responsible decisions as well as for learning mindfully on content of lessons.

 TOC for Education, Inc.

"To make the wish come true..."

TOC for Education, Inc. was established in 1995 as a non-profit foundation to disseminate the logic–based tools and common-sense methodologies in the Theory of Constraints developed for the business world by renowned writer and physicist, Dr. Eliyahu Goldratt (author of "The Goal"). This knowledge is being donated free to education systems worldwide for the purpose of furthering and improving the basis of education provided to students.

The Goal of TOC for Education, Inc. (TOCFE)
The goal is to provide students, educators and parents with dynamic tools that will enable them to accomplish goals, be effective problem-solvers, decision-makers, communicators and life-long learners.

Preface

Putting together this book has been a labour of passion. My 26 years of working with the Ministry of Education, first as a teacher and then as a curriculum developer, have always involved innovative ways of reaching out to children and giving them skills that will last them all their lives.

Discovering the Thinking Processes in the Theory of Constraints for Education (TOCFE) has been a life-changing experience. It is discovering that there is a way to help children learn how to think and not just what to think. It should also not just be for children to go through the motions without involving responsibility. Thinking leads to making responsible decisions be it in terms of content to be learnt or meaningful decisions in your life.

The discovery of these three TOCFE Thinking Tools explored in this book is an eye-opener because they are so simple and concrete that preschool children have used them, right to CEOs in powerful positions! My youngest son, Keenan, has been my TOCFE living laboratory since he was eight and these tools have been tested on many children, teachers and parents who have attended workshops I have conducted not only in Malaysia but also in other parts of the world.

The collection of stories involving a group of teenagers was initially written for a weekly page in *The Next Step*, an Education Supplement in the *News Straits Times*, Malaysia. They were presented in *The Never-Ending Story* from January to May 2004 and for this I wish to thank Datin Rose Ismail for accepting my proposal and New Straits Times Press for granting permission to use the material.

Putting together this collection has involved a wh   ter-
national network of friends at home and abroad. The in   nal
TOCFE community, comprising educational people and
all walks of life, shares whatever it has with the rest of the

I have a special place for Dr Shameem Rafik Gale
kindly agreed to write the Foreword for this book. W
TOCFE may never have been heard in Malaysia. My
especially to Kathy Suerken, President of TOCFE, Inc i1
Florida, who was my first inspiring initiator to the Theory of
Constraints and to Cheryl Edwards of Cedarville, Michigan who
groomed me to be a TOCFE facilitator and changed the course of
my life. Kathy and Cheryl were the original inspiration to "The
Never Ending Story" in USA which started in the year 2000. I have
picked it up to be continued in a Malaysian context.

I wish to express my thanks to several people who have been
behind the public domain material of TOC for Education which
they have generously shared with the world and the special
permission they have given me to put some of the explanations in
print. Thank you to Rami Goldratt for simplifying so many things
effectively and Gila Glatter for sharing her ideas without hesitation
and thank you Linda Trapnell for your original inspiration

I also wish to thank all those who have been instrumental in
helping me develop my interest, those of you whose names I may
not have mentioned and members of my family who have always
supported me in everything I do.

Last but not least, I wish to thank Dr. Eliyahu Goldratt for
sharing and donating the knowledge of the Theory of Constraints
for education to further the cause of education all over the world.

Khaw Choon Ean
Kuala Lumpur

Acknowledgements

The author would like to extend her thanks to:

1. Dr. Eliyahu Goldratt, Kathy Suerken, Cheryl Edwards, Shameem Rafik-Galea, Linda Trapnell, Rami Goldratt, Gila Glatter and all the TOCFE network for the sharing of ideas around the world.
2. The New Straits Times Press (M) Berhad for granting permission to use the material on the Theory of Constraints written for The Next Step between January and May 2004 in this book.
3. Dr. Sharifah Maimunah Syed Zin for her inspiration and support of the Transition Programme launched in 2001
4. Julie Kuan of Subang Jaya for providing some beautiful pictures for the cover of this book.
5. The many beautiful young faces who appear on the cover that are a result of candid shots taken of them in natural moments from visits to schools and friendly shots posed for Julie Kuan.
6. My family members who have been patient and supportive whilst providing valuable feedback for this endeavour

All my friends who have encouraged me in pursuing this passion called TOCFE

Introduction

What is the Theory of Constraints?

Have you heard of the Theory of Constraints (TOC)?

It is based on a world-class management philosophy that focuses on thinking processes developed by well-known writer and physicist, Dr. Eliyahu Goldratt in his book called *The Goal*. But now it can be applied in education from preschool to secondary schools and even in tertiary education.

This book deals with a new approach using simple and clear thinking tools which are concrete and based on logical and systematic thinking. We call it common sense! Intuitive ideas become clearer and can be worded and checked for logic. This can lead to quality communication to convince another person to change for improvement.

How does it help?

Children can be taught to think critically and creatively from a very young age. At the same time, they can also learn to communicate what they are thinking. And not only that, children can also be taught to think logically and systematically with a sense of responsibility.

We want children who learn to think and communicate effectively to show intellectual benchmarks in their thinking. They should make themselves clear. They should show logic and accuracy. They should be able to relate and find relevance in their thinking skills in their daily lives. This, is THINKING SMART.

Three TOC Thinking Tools

TOC tools have been developed for teaching, learning and behaviour development.

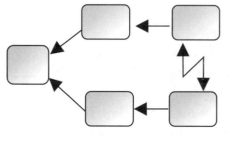

The Evaporating Cloud tool is for looking at conflict situations, be it a personal dilemma, disagreement, argument or even a decision or action that has to be made.

The **Cause and Effect Branch** is for logically thinking through processes or cause and effect from negative behaviour. It allows responsible decisions to be made by looking at predictable consequences and effects. Linking with "If ... then" logic also enables more mindful learning of lesson topics.

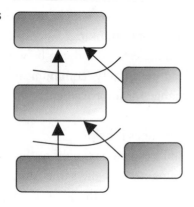

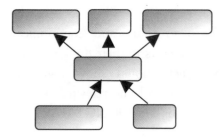

The Ambitious Target Tree tool is for systematic planning, achieving goals set and making an action plan to convert into action every step between the present situation and the goal.

These tools are like graphic organizers and convert complex and messy information collections into meaningful displays. They compress and focus, making interpretations, understanding and insight much easier.

Developments in Malaysia

In 1999, Dr. Shameem Rafik Galea from Universiti Putra Malaysia learnt about the Theory of Constraints For Education (TOCFE) when she attended an International Thinking Conference in Edmonton, Canada. She shared her discovery with the Curriculum Development Centre, Ministry of Education, resulting in a special course presented by Kathy Suerken, CEO and President of TOCFE, Inc., in 2000 to participants from the Ministry of Education.

TOCFE was introduced into Malaysian education through the Transition Programme for Year One students launched by the Ministry of Education in 2001 for all primary schools throughout Malaysia. Using the Theory of Constraints for Education thinking tools as concrete and user-friendly tools for very young children became one of the focus areas of the Transition Programme.

Recently the TOCFE tools have been introduced in the teaching and learning of Social Science subjects and Civics Education in both primary and secondary schools as an innovative methodology in which thinking skills are incorporated in the learning of content, making learning interactive and meaningful and adding relevancy of learning to daily lives.

Developments in Other Countries

TOCFE is used world-wide in at least 20 countries and 3 national education systems. There is also a self-learning package for children as young as six as a course with a multi-user site licence for schools or as a separate single-user CD ROM called The Story of Yani's Goal. TOCFE has also been applied to school peer mediation programmes, promoting leadership skills and even special programmes for gifted children as well as dyslexic children.

To Find Out More

Check out these websites:
www.tocforeducation.com
www.tocforschools.com

The writer can be contacted at khawce@lycos.com

About the Author

 Khaw Choon Ean has always been a trainer, in education and sports as well as in exploring innovative ways to teach and learn as lifelong skills. This has taken her all over the world and throughout Malaysia, sharing what she knows through talks, presentations and workshops. At the same time she dabbles seriously in creative writing, having won many awards in this field. She has run projects in education from thinking skills to multiple intelligences, *orang asli* indigenous education to smart schools and futures studies. Her life's work is to make things simple and explore the most logical way to learn.

A Never-Ending Story...

This is a story of discovery for a group of teenagers
who explore the thinking tools for themselves.
It can be read as a story as well as a learning journey
for anyone who wants to know more about the Theory
of Constraints applied in the context of education and
how these fascinating simple tools can make an impact
in our lives.

CHAPTER 1
Discussing Common Problems

"Hey, Liza!" a high-pitched voice shouted above the din. "What did you do during the long school holidays? Now, tell me what you did for the two months away from school."

Liza smiled at her friends, her face glowing as she spoke, "I actually do have a nice story to share. Something really, really, interesting that you could all learn as well."

"I went to a workshop, a T-O-C Workshop, T-O-C stands for Theory of Constraints. Well, my mum heard of this workshop for youths who would want to learn academic content in a meaningful way, to be responsible decision makers and learn some leadership skills." Liza looked around at her friends who were still listening to her with avid attention. "I learnt to use a set of thinking tools that I can use to help me solve problems."

"Right," said Kah Mun, grinning. "We all have problems, especially at this age. It's a fact we think nobody understands us."

"So are you able to fix problems for everyone now. Liza?" Nurul asked.

"Better than that. I learnt how to fix my own problems and I can teach you how to fix your own, too," Liza said cheerfully.

"What sort of problems do you think we have?" Kah Mun asked. Hadi and Pradesh strode over. The girls smelt a whiff of sweaty uniforms as they approached.

"We heard something about problems. Has anyone got problems over this side?" they asked. "Do we all have the same types of problems?"

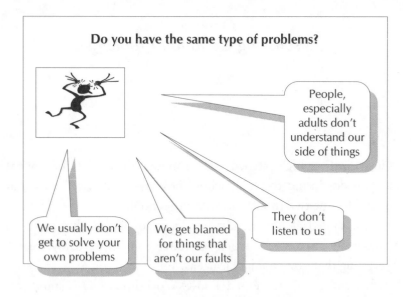

"So Liza," Nurul said, ignoring the boys and turning to her friend, "what have you learnt at the workshop that can help us with a good way of solving problems?"

"Well, we usually don't get to solve our own problems, right? A lot of people will tell you what to do, yet they don't see the other side of things. They get angry when we don't follow what they want us to do." Pradesh said heatedly.

"I feel terrible when I can't solve my problems," Kah Mun said, "It's like I have no control of the situation."

"How does that make you feel?" Liza was smiling calmly at her friends. "So what do we all want to achieve here?"

"It'll be good to be able to know what to do and feel good about it when we encounter problems," said Malliga, looking around at her friends' faces. "Don't we?" They nodded.

Liza whisked out a piece of paper and a pen. She started writing on it. "Well, is that our goal?"

> **OUR GOAL:**
> Feel good about solving problems
> when we encounter them.

"Look, I think this defines our problem on what we have been talking about." Liza tapped her pen on the page she was showing them.

In Liza's notebook ...

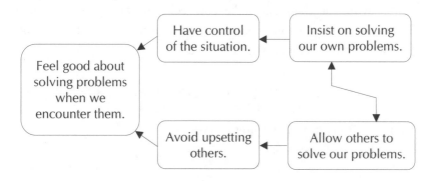

"And like Kah Mun said earlier, in order to feel good we have to have control of the situation and in order to have control of the situation, we insist on solving our own problems," Liza pointed out. "On the other hand," continued Liza, "in order to feel good we don't want to upset others and in order not to upset them we must allow them to solve our problems, that's what you were saying Pradesh, right?"

"That's just right," Hadi interjected, before Pradesh could answer.

"Looks like this shows why we feel having problems is such a frustrating thing. We are caught between insisting on solving our own problems and allowing others to do it for us. It looks like we are in a never-ending conflict situation," Liza said.

"But now things will change," she declared, giving her friends a nod and a 'thumbs-up' sign.

"So we are going to solve that problem you have mapped out so nicely?" asked Malliga. "Did you learn that at the workshop?"

"That's right, I did. And we can look at that problem together."

"Goodness, first day of school and we are already talking about problems. Aren't we a cheerful lot?" said Kah Mun, as the others laughed at her comment.

"Not to worry, everyone. I am going to share some good things with you that will make you feel good about yourselves," Liza said, as they fell in line, two-by-two on the way to the school hall where the assembly would be held.

IT'S YOUR TURN TO THINK ...

Can You Think of Other Types of Problems?

CHAPTER 2
Understanding the Meaning of Conflict

The next time they got together was at recess.

They moved to a quiet part of the school complex, to one of the small cosy gazebos that had been built for reading corners. They agreed to sit there after letting Hadi and Pradesh know where they could find them. Malliga shared out her box of *vadai* and they smelt so good that Nurul was tempted to break her new year resolution immediately.

"Can we get back to that thing you drew this morning, about our common problems?" Kah Mun asked after they had finished their portions of *vadai*. Liza took out her notebook from her pocket.

"Looks like these two sides want different things," Nurul said pointing to the boxes on the right. "Is that why you joined the two boxes with zigzag arrows?"

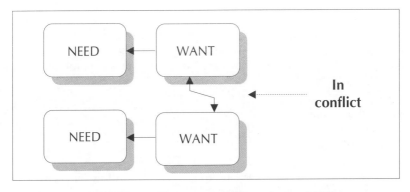

Lisa nodded, "A conflict is normally a clash of different wants. Insisting on solving our own problems is in conflict with allowing

5

others to solve our problems. You can't have both at the same time."

Nurul continued tracing her finger across the diagram. "And there are a set of straight arrows leading from those boxes on the right to the middle boxes."

Liza pointed to the boxes on the far right. "Those boxes show our wants that are in conflict, and the linking arrows from each box show the link to the next box which shows the needs." Liza started writing in her notebook again.

"So each side has a want that is the result of a need?"

"You're getting the picture," Liza said, showing the new boxes she had drawn. "See the arrows linking the wants and needs. When we insist on getting a certain 'want' we always have a reason … a 'need'."

"So *in order to be in control of the situation* is our need or reason for insisting we solve our own problems? Hmm, sounds logical. And *in order to avoid upsetting others* is the reason or need for allowing them to solve our problems for us?" Liza told them, reading from the diagram.

"So Liza, this means you are describing our problem using this diagram."

In Liza's notebook ...

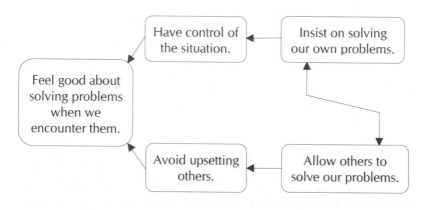

6

Liza's said ...

> In order to feel good we have to have control of the situation and in order to have control of the situation, we insist on solving our own problems. On the other hand, in order to feel good we don't want to upset others and in order not to upset them we must allow them to solve our problems.

"Yes, this one describes a personal dilemma, an internal conflict. If it describes a problem between two people then it is an external conflict. It could be a disagreement, an argument, a quarrel."

"So in our personal dilemma or problems, if I insist on the WANT of one side, like we insist on solving our own problems, the other side will not get its NEED, meaning we upset people who want to solve problems for us," Pradesh said, looking thoughtful. "I'm getting the logic."

"And vice versa for the other side insisting on its WANT," said Liza.

"So what if we can describe the problem using this way?"

"If you understand and can define a problem you are halfway to solving it. Otherwise, when you can see the conflict of different WANTS and each side keeps insisting on getting its want, it will be like a never-ending story."

"So how now?" asked Hadi, scratching his head.

"That's why we have to find out each side's NEEDs because we can give up what we WANT if we can satisfy our original needs in another way." Liza told her friends.

"But which side is right or wrong?"

"Must there always be a right or wrong? Okay, we have to be getting back to the class now. I'll tell you more next time. I promise you I will share what I have learnt at my workshop ... how to solve problems in a fair way using TOC."

"TOC?"

"I told you this morning ... Theory of Constraints."

They all started walking back to class, Liza striding ahead and looking back at her friends.

IT'S YOUR TURN TO THINK...

Let's Just Practise the Idea of 'Wants' and 'Needs'

Below is an example of a situation. See how in the same situation there can be two sides wanting different things. Liza says this is because there is a different reason for each 'want'.

Storyline:

Malliga brought some delicious *vadai* (Indian cakes) to school. Nurul has made a new year's resolution not to eat snacks in between her main meals.

Try to define the different WANTS in this situation. Asking "WHY" will determine the real reasons for the conflict.

Question: **Who is having the problem?**

Answer: **Nurul.** She has a decision to make.

Question: **What is Nurul's problem?**

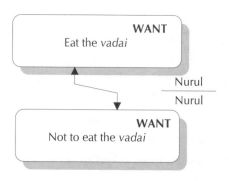

8

Defining Nurul's Problem

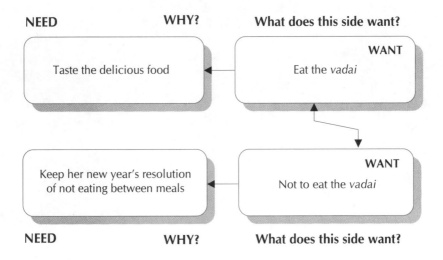

Communicating Nurul's Problem

In order to ... *(NEED)* ..., Nurul must ... *(WANT)* ...
In order to ... *(NEED)* ..., Nurul must not ... *(WANT)* ...
In order to *taste the delicious food*, Nurul must *eat the vadai.*
In order to *keep her new year's resolution of not eating between meals*; Nurul must not eat the *vadai.*

Is there a right or wrong decision here?

Who's to Blame?

They could only get together again the following day. Hadi was eager to corner Liza so that he could get her to answer his last question. She'd described the problem using her boxes and arrows. They put the problem in a logical and clear manner but he still wanted to know which side was right or wrong.

"Then which is right or wrong?" asked Hadi, stopping Liza as she walked past him to her seat that morning. "If between two different persons, I would always think that my side is right so how are we going to decide?"

Hadi was keen to know because he was always in some sort of trouble or other with his teachers or friends and he always said he was right and they were wrong.

"Does it always have to be a wrong and a right side?" asked Liza.

"Well, I suppose we can look at the same problem and see it differently, but nobody's wrong," Nurul said reasonably from where she was sitting.

Lisa started to flick through her notebook in an excited manner. "You're right, Nurul. Let me show you this picture, what do you see?"

"I see an old man," Pradesh said promptly, "an old man with a big moustache."

"I see an old lady with a crooked nose," claimed Malliga.

"What old lady?" Hadi said. "I don't see an old man or an old lady. I see a pretty young lady with a fur-collared dress." He took the notebook from Liza and put it in front of his nose. "Nope, still can't see any old lady or old man."

Nurul wrestled the notebook from Hadi's hands and took a good look.

"Actually, Liza, I can see all three!"

"That's what I meant," said Liza. "It's the same picture. But here, let me show you." She traced the profile of the old lady. "If you follow this you will see the old lady's profile and the old man's."

But Liza continued speaking. "Each one of you saw different things from the same picture. Is any one of you wrong?"

"No, we were just seeing what we thought we saw. Like being just one-sided, I guess," replied Pradesh, "certainly not wrong."

"Exactly," Liza said. "Sometimes we just fix on one point and claim we are right."

"Where did you get that picture from, Liza?" asked Malliga. "It's a great way of making your point. Now I can see what you mean when you said it doesn't always have to be right or wrong. It's just how we see something."

"I got it from my holiday workshop. They used it at the workshop to show why we should listen to the other side when we have a problem."

"Nobody wants to listen to the other side," Hadi grumbled. He knew what he was saying because he was always in some conflict with somebody.

"Why is that so?" asked Liza.

"Each side is always too busy trying to blame each other."

"But if the other side is the one at fault, how can we give in to what he or she wants?" asked Kah Mun who had been thoughtful and quiet all this while. "It won't be fair!"

"Well, if you keep blaming each other, will you ever solve a problem?" Liza asked. "How do you feel when you get blamed in a situation?"

"I'll feel terrible!"

"I'll feel stupid and embarrassed."

"Or humiliated."

"I hate it when I am asked to apologise when I feel I am right."

"So we seem to agree that putting blame makes everyone feel awful. So why do we still solve problems by blaming the other side when we know it makes the situation worse and it doesn't really solve the problem?" Liza asked earnestly.

"Hey, ask me, I know," said Hadi, grinning as he brushed back some of his hair that had fallen over his eyes. "If I don't blame someone, I will get blamed!" Knowing Hadi's history of problems, everyone chuckled good-naturedly.

The bell rang and the Geography teacher, Mrs Rohani, was already at the door with a pile of papers. They quickly got back to their seats. But Liza was able to whisper to Hadi before the lesson started.

"And, no one gets blamed in fixing problems the TOC way," said Liza looking meaningfully at Hadi.

IT'S YOUR TURN TO THINK ...

Why is it Important to see Both Sides of the Problem?

What Can You See?

There is always emotion attached to a conflict. It is very easy to blame someone for a problem. It would be better if this emotion is focused on getting to a **solution**. In other words, we turn the situation from 'you against me' to "you and me against the problem".

A TOC cloud tool enables a student to really listen with an **open mind** to **both sides** of the problem in a way that creates not only self-awareness but also empathy for the other side. This ensures the feelings of both sides are treated with **respect**.

Is Whatever You can see Right or Wrong?

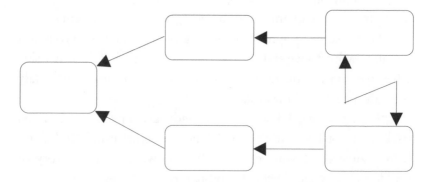

The **Evaporating Cloud** tool is for looking at conflict situations. It is used to clearly and precisely identify and define the problem *without* casting blame.

Is There a Right or Wrong Decision Here?

Hadi has asked Pradesh to go see a movie with him. They have a Geography test the next day and Hadi wants to relax before the test.

Pradesh is worried that he is not ready for the test and needs the time to study.

Here is problem of differing wants. Both Hadi and Pradesh have important NEEDs.

Who are the two sides involved?
The two parties in this situation are ... and ...
What does each side want? Why?

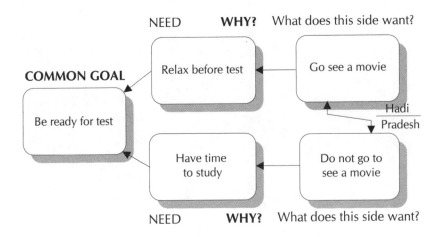

If Hadi can have his NEED and Pradesh can have his NEED fulfilled, what COMMON GOAL will be achieved?

Let's define the problem here:
In order to … (COMMON GOAL) …, Hadi … (NEED) …
In order to … (NEED) …, Hadi wants to … (WANT) …

On the other hand,
In order to … (COMMON GOAL) …, Pradesh … (NEED) …
In order to … (NEED) …, Pradesh does not want to (NEED) …

Defining the problem clearly:
In order to *be ready for the test*, Hadi needs *to relax before the test*.
In order to *relax before his test*, Hadi wants *to go see a movie*.

On the other hand,
In order to *be ready for the test*, Pradesh needs to *have time to study*.
In order to *have time to study*, Pradesh *does not go to see a movie*.

QUESTION:
Can you say Hadi is wrong or Pradesh is right?
Or can you say Pradesh is wrong and Hadi is right?

CHAPTER 4
Empowering Each Person

The mathematics lesson was just over. Liza heard a commotion at the back of the class. She looked up in time to see Hadi and Ruzain, the class monitor, glaring at and confronting each other. Ruzain's hand was on the switches for the fans, turning them on. Hadi was trying to get to the switches to switch them off.

The next teacher had not come in yet. Liza walked over to the back, sizing up the situation. Ruzain was trying to look imposing, putting on his 'class monitor' face and Hadi looked rebellious.

"Hey, guys, what's the matter?" Liza asked. "Can I help?"

"I want the fans turned off," said Hadi, looking accusingly at Ruzain.

"It's almost noon and the classroom is warm. As class monitor, I should see that everyone else feels comfortable." He looked at the old ceiling fans as they turned round cooling the hot air in the room.

"I don't like the fan on because it messes up my hair."

"You shouldn't be selfish," said Ruzain. "And vain," he added, after a pause.

"So I'm the one to be accused again, as usual," Hadi said, raising his voice. The others in the class were backing away. No one liked a quarrel.

Liza asked again, louder this time. "Calm down, let's see what the real problem is here."

The two boys looked at her as if she was mad.

"Isn't the problem obvious?" asked Ruzain. "I want to have the fans switched on and he doesn't. We are arguing. I want one thing and he wants another."

"That's how a problem starts, Ruzain, Hadi," Liza said looking from one to the other. "Usually it's a disagreement between two people because both can't have what they want at the same time."

"So who is to be blamed?" asked Ruzain.

"No one," said Liza. "We can look at the start of your problem and we need not point fingers at anyone. Obviously you both have your reasons for quarrelling over the fan." Hadi remembered the time Liza had explained to a few of them about not blaming each other as a way of fixing problems.

"Look, you can deal with this situation better if you understand why each of you wants something different. It's not a case of Hadi versus Ruzain."

Kah Mun shouted from the front of the class, "I'll write your problem on the board," she volunteered, taking a piece of chalk and writing on the board. "The two sides involved are Ruzain and Hadi," she said, writing the two names down. "I'm adding the zigzag arrow to show it's a conflict of wants."

The whole class' attention was now on Kah Mun at the blackboard, wondering what she was doing, especially those who had no idea about Liza attending a problem-solving workshop and teaching a few classmates what she had learnt.

Liza smiled to herself as she saw Kah Mun writing on the board. She turned to the two boys. "Right, Ruzain, why did you want the fans switched on?"

"To make the classroom cooler."

"And why don't you want them switched on, Hadi?"

"To prevent my hair from getting messed up when the fan is blowing. I like my hair tidy."

"You've got that, Kah Mun?"

"Yes, I have. And I'm adding the arrows to show the link, right, Liza?"

Everyone was staring at the diagram Kah Mun was writing on the board.

"What are you doing?" asked Eng Joo, a stout boy who was sitting in front.

"Defining their problem," Kah Mun replied smugly. "Helping them solve it, I hope."

"Now we ask what will be achieved if Ruzain can keep the class cool and Hadi's hair doesn't get messed up?" Liza waited for an answer, and turning to Kah Mun, instructed. "Kah Mun, put two arrows from the boxes for NEEDs and add one box where they lead."

"Come on, tell us what we achieve if both of them get what they need."

"A good day at school?" suggested Eng Joo. A few people said "Yes!" to that so Kah Mun wrote it down. Then Kah Mun, Ruzain and Hadi went back to their seats.

What Kah Mun wrote on the blackboard ...

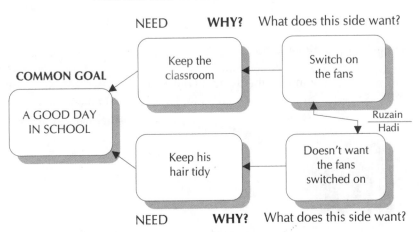

19

Only Liza was standing up.

She was reading from the blackboard.

"*In order to have a good day at school, Ruzain wants to keep the classroom cool. In order to keep the classroom cool, he switches on the fans. On the other hand, in order to have a good day in school, Hadi wants to keep his hair tidy. In order to keep his hair tidy, he doesn't want the fans switched on.* How does that sound?"

"Well said," Nurul applauded, clapping her hands, "so how do we solve their problem?"

Of course the next teacher chose to walk into the class at that moment. Mrs. Ganapathy, the English Language teacher looked from the diagram on the board to the faces of the students.

"What's going on?" she demanded to know. The whole class turned their faces towards Liza, waiting for her to answer.

"Empowering ourselves to solve a problem, Mrs. Ganapathy," she said, confidently.

IT'S YOUR TURN TO THINK ...

Write out what Liza said:

In order to ....
....
On the other hand, in order to ....
....

Dealing with Conflict

The whole class stood up and chorused, "Good morning, teacher," and sat down to the noisy scrapping of chair legs on the floor.

"What's this?" the teacher asked, pointing to the cloud diagram.

"It's called a TOC cloud, teacher," Liza explained politely. "It's a thinking tool I learnt at a workshop to help define a problem so that people will look at the problem and try to solve it instead of fighting with each other."

What Kah Mun wrote on the blackboard ...

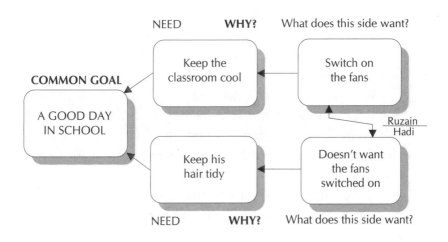

"TOC cloud? I've never heard of that," the teacher said. "What does TOC stand for?"

"Theory of Constraints, a logical and systematic thinking strategy for problem solving."

"Hmmm, looks interesting, "she said, staring at the Cloud diagram on the board. "I suppose Ruzain and Hadi were having a fight over the fans as usual before I came in?" A few students laughed.

"Okay, Liza. Since so much trouble has been taken to draw this on the board, would you like to explain a little?" Liza stood up and beamed. "I'd love to." She heard a few groaning sounds especially from a group of boys. Ruzain sat tight-lipped and Hadi still looked annoyed.

Liza started telling the class how a situation could always become a problem when there were two sides involved that had opposite wants that they couldn't have simultaneously. She also explained about needs which were usually the reason behind why a person  wanted something. So a conflict problem was usually a clash of wants.

"A conflict gets bad when each side refuses to give up their want." Liza said.

"What do you mean by 'gets bad'?" asked Mrs. Ganapathy.

"The situation deteriorates, teacher, unless they can solve the problem in a way acceptable to both sides, which is to focus on satisfying the NEEDs or the real reasons on each side for insisting on what they want."

"So you mean to say that using this TOC Cloud tool will empower a person to solve his or her own conflict problems?" asked Mrs. Ganapathy.

"Yes, teacher."

Kah Mun put up her hand. "Yes. Kah Mun?" Mrs. Ganapathy asked, peering at her over her glasses.

"We haven't solved the problem yet, teacher. Could we ask Liza to finish teaching us how to deal with this conflict?"

Mrs. Ganapathy looked at her watch. "All right, we have some time to spare which I was going to use to get all of you engaged in a Question and Answer activity, so this will replace that." She sat down on her chair. "Liza, please continue."

"Well, before we can solve this conflict we have to understand how we normally deal with conflicts." Liza explained. Eng Joo, the chubby classmate sitting in front, put up his hand. "Can I ask a question?" Liza looked at him waiting for the question.

"You mean there are normal and NOT normal ways?" he asked.

Liza shook her head. "How do we usually solve conflicts?" Liza asked. "Look at the present problem between Ruzain and Hadi. If Ruzain insists on getting what he wants, Ruzain will be imposing on Hadi, so Hadi will feel that he 'loses' because he has to give in to Ruzain's wishes and will he be happy then?"

"If Hadi gets to switch off the fan, Ruzain 'loses' and how does he feel?"

"He's the monitor. He will feel as if Hadi had over-ruled his decision as a leader," Nurul pointed out.

"Right. So they may continue with a tug-of-war situation ... ON-OFF ... ON-OFF ... ON-OFF ... big struggle."

"They could compromise," said Malliga, looking at the teacher who was listening attentively. "Hadi could have some time without the fan and Ruzain could have some time with the fan on."

Liza again shook her head. "A compromise won't solve the problem because their real reasons are not looked after. Having the fan turned on or off is just an expression of their real reasons or needs. So whenever the fan is on, Hadi's need of keeping his hair tidy will always be unfulfilled. It's like a half-solution."

"This is terrible," Mrs. Ganapathy spoke up, "So Liza you are saying we cannot have a tug-of-war nor impose, we cannot give in and we cannot compromise? Then how do we solve the problem?"

"Can we pretend that there is no conflict? Not talk about it? Don't take any sides?" asked Eng Joo.

"Oh no," Liza said, "that's avoidance and hiding from a problem doesn't make it go away."

"Then what can we do?" asked Ruzain gruffly, obviously piqued and unhappy.

"In the TOC Workshop, we were taught to provide Win-Win solutions!"

"Win-Win?" asked Hadi, sitting up, "now, I'd like that. We can only have win-win if I can keep my hair tidy and Ruzain gets to keep this classroom cool, right?"

"You're getting to it, Hadi," Liza said.

"I'm afraid time's up, Liza," said the English teacher. "Class, you will need to find out your win-win later. Right, we have to look at phrasal verbs today." The class groaned.

"Right, thank you, Liza. I hope the rest of the class has been listening. Ruzain, Hadi ... you can see Liza after class to solve your conflict with a win-win solution. Meanwhile, I'd like to start my lesson."

"It was getting exciting," protested Nurul.

"A problem well-defined is halfway solved"
Theory of Constraints
When we empower ourselves with the skills to deal with our own problems, we must first of all learn how to define our problem in a clear and fair way that does not blame anyone.

IT'S YOUR TURN TO THINK...

The Common Goal or Common Objective

This is a situation desired by both sides, if the conflict can be resolved.

When you are in a conflict situation you may not realise that there is a common situation both sides actually would like to achieve.

This can be done basically by letting both sides have their needs. For example, in the class incident, if Hadi's need was to keep his hair tidy and if he gets his need to keep his hair tidy, he will not fight over the fans being switched on. The real need for Ruzain was to make the classroom cooler and if this need could be met, then he will not be fighting over wanting the fans to be switched on.

So even though the common goal is not a solution in itself, knowing there is a common objective can increase the desire to find a solution itself.

We're sure there is something we would like to achieve in common.

Common Ways of Dealing with Conflict

These are the common ways of dealing with conflict.

Match the situations in the boxes on the right with the pictures on the left.

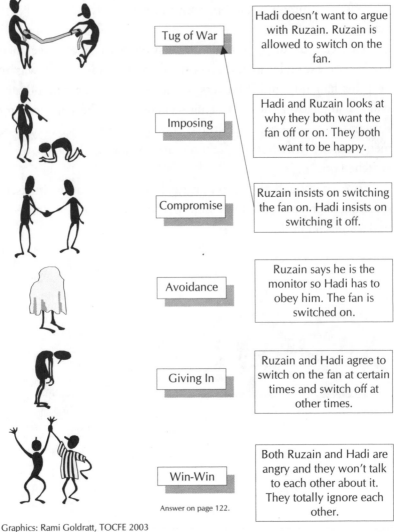

Tug of War

Hadi doesn't want to argue with Ruzain. Ruzain is allowed to switch on the fan.

Imposing

Hadi and Ruzain looks at why they both want the fan off or on. They both want to be happy.

Compromise

Ruzain insists on switching the fan on. Hadi insists on switching it off.

Avoidance

Ruzain says he is the monitor so Hadi has to obey him. The fan is switched on.

Giving In

Ruzain and Hadi agree to switch on the fan at certain times and switch off at other times.

Win-Win

Both Ruzain and Hadi are angry and they won't talk to each other about it. They totally ignore each other.

Answer on page 122.

Graphics: Rami Goldratt, TOCFE 2003

Both Sides Now

"We haven't solved the problem between Ruzain and Hadi," Kah Mun reminded Liza, "When are you going to do it?"

"To understand Win-Win they should know what they want to achieve when they solve their problem." Liza replied. From where they were sitting, they could see Ruzain and Hadi approaching.

"What do you mean?" asked Malliga and the others also looked questioningly at Liza.

"Let's ask them," Liza said, smiling at all of them as the two boys reached them.

"Hi, guys. I know, I know, you're going to ask about Win-Win!" Liza said, putting up her hand as the two boys were about to say something. Kah Mun passed her the paper where she had earlier copied down the conflict definition of the problem from the board.

"First of all, let's ask again what both of you will achieve if you are both satisfied over the issue of the ceiling fans," said Liza.

"I thought we've got that down," said Kah Mun, jabbing a finger at what she'd written on the paper.

"Right, but they have to agree that it is what they desire to have," explained Liza. "Then they can work towards this common goal for a Win-Win solution. Okay, guys?"

"So, you have already put our common goal as a good day in school, haven't you?" Ruzain said pointing to Kah Mun's diagram.

"So how are you going to have this good day at school?" asked Malliga, fluttering her hands at them.

"When we get what's important to us!" Hadi said strongly.

"That's right," said Liza, "The new way of thinking in TOC or 'Theory of Constraints' way of thinking Win-Win is to aim for a situation where you both get what you need."

"In other words," said Nurul, pretending to talk like a wise old sage, "you don't want to fight over the ceiling fans but to see that Ruzain gets the class cool and Hadi keeps his hair tidy."

"Nicely put, Nurul," Kah Mun said, joining in the fun of pretending to talk like a wise old sage.

"Hang on a moment," said Malliga raising a hand, "what exactly can they do so that Ruzain can keep the class cool and Hadi keeps his hair tidy?"

"That's exactly it!" exclaimed Liza. "We have to aim for a Win-Win meaning, how do we give them both what is important as a need for both of them?"

"So, as they both have such differing wants, we can't rely on giving what each of them *wants* but we can see whether there are other ways they can get their *need*!" Malliga said, punching the air in an unladylike manner, "Hah, how can we do that, hmmm, very interesting."

"Aha, I see a new way of thinking, this thinking in Win-Win." said Nurul, in her wise man's voice.

Liza was immensely pleased how her friends seemed to be catching on the whole idea of thinking win-win. "So Ruzain and Hadi had a problem and we defined that problem properly in a cloud. That's Step One. Step Two, we need to shift their focus from what they want to what is important to them, their REASON for wanting the fan on or off and Step Three, we think of different ways of giving them what's important."

"So it looks like we need a way to keep the classroom cool which doesn't mess up Hadi's hair," summed up Ruzain, "Or some way of keeping Hadi's hair tidy that will allow me to keep the classroom cool. It doesn't look that easy to find a Win-Win for this."

"Hey, think again," Liza said. "As long as we are going through the steps of defining the problem with giving a fair look at BOTH sides, then shifting our focus to your NEEDs, we are already using a Win-Win approach. Now, that remains the last step to tackle."

"The last step?" asked Hadi, "What's that, Liza?"

"I just said it. The last step in the Win-Win way is to look for other ways you can get what you need and not necessary through switching on or off the fans. Maybe when we examine the problem so nicely put in that cloud, one of you might like the alternative way better than fighting over the fan."

"Eh, better said than done," said Nurul. "So we have given a look at both sides and know they both want a common desirable situation, but how do we get them to get to agree on something when the whole problem was because they couldn't agree in the first place?"

"That's the whole problem. What we need is to think out of the box."

"What box?" asked Hadi, looking confused.

"Never mind that for the moment," Liza said, laughingly. "I'll let you guys think over alternative ways to get your needs fulfilled. Next time we meet I'll explain about thinking outside the box, okay?"

"Hey, do I need to carry a box ready for when we next get together?" asked Hadi with a grin.

"You great joker!" said Nurul and Malliga did her fluttering hands gesture at him again.

"And don't forget about the win-win steps I explained just now," Liza called out to the boys as the girls walked off in the opposite direction from the boys.

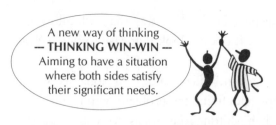

A new way of thinking
— **THINKING WIN-WIN** —
Aiming to have a situation
where both sides satisfy
their significant needs.

IT'S YOUR TURN TO THINK ...

STEP **1**   **Analyze The Problem in a Fair Way.**

The CLOUD is a logical thinking tool we use in order to analyze a conflict situation.

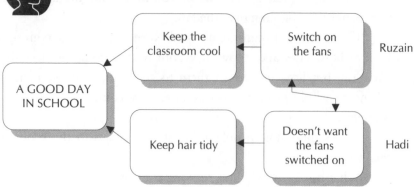

- The broken arrow symbolises the conflict – you cannot have both WANTS at the same time.
- The NEED is the reason why each side insists on getting what he wants. In order to make sure each side gets his NEED, it is necessary to achieve what he WANTs.
- The COMMON GOAL is a situation both sides wish to have, but in order to reach that, each side must get his NEED.

STEP 2 | **Shift the Focus from the Wants to the Needs.**

- A Win-Win solution is a solution that enables both sides to satisfy their significant Needs.
- The problem is that in order to satisfy the Needs each side insists on getting conflicting Wants.
- Thinking Win-Win requires us to shift the focus from striving to get what we want, to striving to satisfy our needs.

STEP 3 |
- In order to have a Win-Win solution at least one side will have to find an alternative way to satisfy the Need.

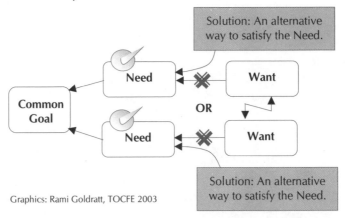

Graphics: Rami Goldratt, TOCFE 2003

Think of a conflict situation between friends in your classroom. Write the storyline.
- Who are involved in the conflict?
- Define the problem in a cloud.
- Use Steps 1 to 3 to try and solve the problem in a Win-Win approach.

31

CHAPTER 7
Thinking Out of the Box

"Here they come," Kah Mun said looking at Ruzain and Hadi walking towards them, "I told you they do want to settle their dispute together. That's good, isn't it?"

"When they are ready to agree their needs are more important than their wants, they are ready to find their solution." Liza replied.

"We are ready to think out of the box!" Hadi announced, "How do we start?"

Liza turned to Ruzain who was looking very serious. "Important question here is, Ruzain, do you find it more important to switch on the fans or to keep the classroom cool?"

Ruzain shook his head. "The only reason I want the fans switched on is because the classroom is warm and needs cooling." Liza nodded. "So that's important to you, Ruzain. And you Hadi?"

"Of course it is more important for me to keep my hair tidy, that's why I am insisting on switching off the fans because the draught starts messing up my hair!"

"Then would it be a problem to allow the fans to be switched on, if you can keep your hair tidy?"

"I suppose not," Hadi replied, sulkily. "But I don't see how, if the fans are switched on."

"Hmmm, you need to keep your hair tidy so you want the fans switched off. Think, is there another way to keep your hair tidy?"

"I could use more hair gel or cream, I suppose," Hadi said, slowly.

"Or change to an update, funkier short hairstyle that won't get blown by wind draughts," suggested Nurul, clutching both hands to the sides of her head, to illustrate her description.

"Or sit at a place which is not directly under the fan," Kah Mun said. "I'll swap places with you."

"So you see, Hadi," said Liza, "that's exactly what I mean. If we can have other ways to keep our important need we need not insist on wanting just one way of meeting that need. There can be other different ways, not just switching off the fan."

"Ahhh, like thinking out of the box, not just in a narrow way. Not always easy, you know," said Malliga, looking at Hadi who seemed to be thinking about all the suggestions.

"That's right, Malliga." Liza agreed. "And you sound like you have attended my TOC workshop too!"

Malliga looked pleased. "Really? Well, I guess that's because the thinking process is so logical."

"I learnt at the workshop that you can sometimes easily find other ways to get what's important to you instead of just insisting on one thing. Of course not always easy but we have to learn to think out of the box."

"If you don't mind," Kah Mun said, "I don't quite understand about this 'think-out-of-the-box' business. What do you mean?"

"Here, I can illustrate by using this puzzle." Liza started drawing an arrangement of dots on the paper Kah Mun was holding. All the others crowded around her, looking over her shoulder.

"Now, can you join all these nine dots using four straight lines, without lifting your pencil, without retracing any lines?" asked Liza as she passed the paper to Hadi and Ruzain. Everyone started giving advice and a lot of pencil marks were made and then rubbed out.

"Here, let me show you," Nurul said, taking the pencil. "See, one, two, three, four … there!" The others stared in amazement at her effort.

"You got it because you drew outside the formation!" exclaimed Hadi, almost like an accusation.

"Now, now, well done, Nurul!" Liza said, clucking like Mrs. Ganapathy, the English teacher. "THAT's thinking outside the box! You all thought or ASSUMED you couldn't go outside the formation. No one said we should stick within only ONE way to solve a puzzle. Just like our problems."

"You mean TOC teaches you that?"

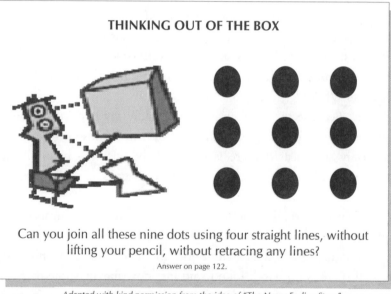

THINKING OUT OF THE BOX

Can you join all these nine dots using four straight lines, without lifting your pencil, without retracing any lines?

Answer on page 122.

Adapted with kind permission from the idea of "The Never-Ending Story"
(Suerken and Edwards, TOCFE, Inc, 2000)

"More difficult than we thought," muttered Ruzain.

"Yes! To help us think out of the box using the TOC Cloud we have a way of asking questions for thinking about the link between saying what you WANT and WHY you want that. Like this …"

Liza drew her boxes and put a line in between the arrow linking WANT and NEED.

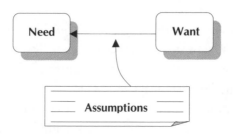

"In the cloud diagram, we call it an ASSUMPTION, or the reason you assume that only a particular thing that you WANT can meet the important NEED you have," explained Liza.

Hadi and the others looked puzzled. Liza took Kah Mun's cloud diagram and shook it out for her friends to see. "Right, let me put it this way, Hadi, your side says: In order to keep your hair tidy, you must switch off the ceiling fans because ... well, tell us ... because WHY?"

"... Because the wind draught will blow my hair into a mess, because my hair is long enough to be blown, because my hairstyle can only stay neat if there is no wind, because my hair will be blown out of place where I am sitting ... because ... well, I could go on."

"Can you think whether any one of those assumptions is untrue?"

"Hmm, I guess that assumption about my hair can only stay neat if there is no wind. Like I said just now maybe some hair gel or cream can hold it firmly in place or like Nurul says, I could get a shorter hairstyle. There's no reason I need to keep this particular hairstyle. Or swap places with Kah Mun."

"If you find any assumption untrue and no longer valid, THAT becomes your SOLUTION as you have proven by coming up with those suggestions which you can follow instead of quarrelling over the fans with Ruzain, In TOC, that's thinking out of the box," said

Liza triumphantly. "After all, tidy hair is more important to you than a fight over switching the fans on or off."

IT'S YOUR TURN TO THINK ...

TRYING TO FIND WIN-WIN SOLUTIONS SYSTEMATICALLY

Does each side continue to insist on getting what he wants without a reason?

Each side can explain why the Want is necessary to satisfy the Need. These explanations are ASSUMPTIONS that each side makes.

Surfacing and examining these assumptions may lead one of the sides to the realization that he can satisfy the Need without getting the Want.

In order to satisfy my need I must have what I want because ... [Assumptions] ...

In order to surface the assumptions we have to find out why getting the Want is necessary to fulfill the Need.

Then we examine each assumption to know if it is really valid, and whether we can do something to make it invalid.

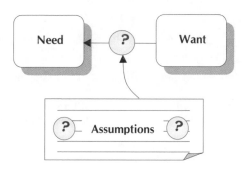

Graphics: Rami Goldratt, TOCFE 2003

HADI'S ASSUMPTIONS:

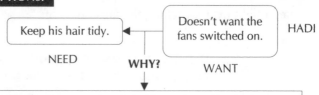

| Keep his hair tidy. | ◄─── | Doesn't want the fans switched on. | HADI |

NEED   **WHY?**   WANT

Assumptions:
Because the wind draught will blow my hair into a mess
Because my hair is long enough to be blown
Because my hairstyle can only stay neat if there is no wind
Because my hair will be blown out of place where I am sitting

Invalid ASSUMPTION
Because my hairstyle can only stay neat if there is no wind.

ALTERNATIVE SUGGESTIONS to Keep Hair Tidy
Use hair gel or hair cream
Change to a shorter hairstyle

TRY TO HELP RUZAIN THINK OF A WIN-WIN SOLUTION

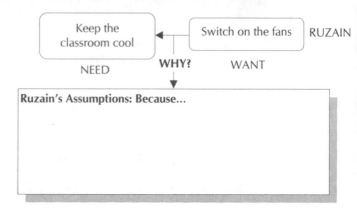

| Keep the classroom cool | ◄─── | Switch on the fans | RUZAIN |

NEED   **WHY?**   WANT

Ruzain's Assumptions: Because...

Any Invalid Assumption?

Alternative Suggestions to keep Classroom Cool

CHAPTER 8
Changing Behaviour, Examining Needs

Graphics: Rami Goldratt, TOCFE 2003

The next time Mrs. Ganapathy came to their class, she looked immediately at the whirring ceiling fans and noted that Hadi had a new shorter hairstyle and had swapped places with Kah Mun.

"I see that you have all reached a win-win situation," she commented and Liza and Nurul gave her a 'thumbs up' gesture. Hadi looked a little embarrassed but smiled and Ruzain gave a brief nod.

"They're having a good day in school,' said chubby Eng Joo pleasantly. The class laughed at this.

"This seems to be a good approach to look at problems then." Mrs. Ganapathy said. "You're not fighting over the fan, finally. And Hadi looks quite good with his new hairstyle." Hadi's face beamed.

Mrs. Ganapathy walked to the front, facing the class. "This shows me that we can change our behaviour and stop fighting by looking at what is important to us, our needs. I'm going to suggest we have a class lesson on this. Then everyone will be able to look at their own problems and solve them in a good and responsible way. What do you think?"

There was a general chorus of 'okays' and 'yes!'. Some boys even beat the top their tables to show approval. "Right then," said Mrs. Ganapathy. "Liza and her friends can explain the process."

Liza proceeded to explain, with Kah Mun and Malliga at the blackboard drawing the structure of the Cloud and Nurul was asked to explain about win-win and thinking outside the box. Liza asked Hadi and Ruzain to define and communicate their problem using the cloud. Their friends listened attentively.

Then Pradesh raised his hand, "I have a question," he said, "what sort of problems do we look at with this TOC cloud thinking process?"

"Day-to-day problems are good for this approach. You know those that involve conflict and bother us but are not too complicated or deep-set ones. Problems will get worse if we don't fix them."

"Right then," Mrs. Ganapathy said, stepping forward to take over. "Thank you Liza and team. I am going to ask all of you to try using this thinking process now. We will start, I think, by identifying some examples of simple day-to-day conflicts." She walked to the board. "I'll give you a few minutes to think about this or discuss with your friend sitting beside you."

A while later, Mrs. Ganapathy said, "Right, now can I have any examples of day-to-day conflicts?" Her chalk was poised to write them down. A lot of waving hands shot up.

"A friend wants to borrow my computer game and I don't want to lend it."

"My best friend wants to copy my project and I want her to do her own work."

"I want to go to a friend's party and my mum doesn't want me to go."

"Eng Joo wants to join our soccer team but we don't want him because he is not a good player."

"I want Ratna to go to the shopping mall with me but she doesn't want to."

Mrs. Ganapathy wrote everything in a list on the board. She told the class, "This is a good list of day-to-day problems you all usually face. Now what do we do next with them?"

"We can write out a brief storyline and then we define the conflicts in a cloud structure, asking whether this is an internal or external conflict and what are the two sides involved," Liza said. "Then we write the exact conflict as a set of opposite WANTs, using a zigzag arrow."

"Good, class, work in pairs and choose one of the conflicts on the list or one you have. Take out your Composition exercise books and write the storyline for the problem and follow the steps I'm writing on the board." The humming sound of voices in lively discussion started.

After a few minutes, Liza could see her friends were ready to proceed. "May I continue, teacher?" she asked. "Now we have to put the reasons each side is insisting on the want. Draw a box to the left of the conflict box. Use an arrow to connect between the two boxes."

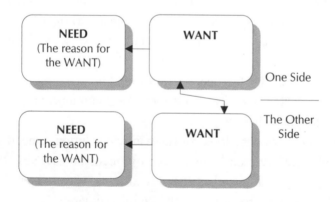

"Done!" said Eng Joo. "What next?"

"Then in the boxes on the left, put in the important reason why each side is insisting on their WANTS. Why do they want that?"

41

"Now two arrows from the NEEDs link to the fifth box which is the desirable situation both sides achieve if they get their needs. It should be a POSITIVE statement because this is the common goal both sides would want to have if they solve the problem."

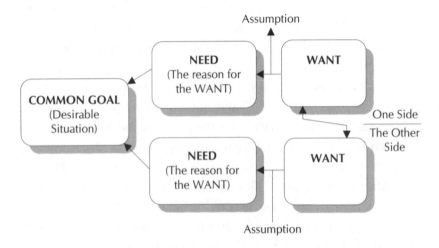

"Now we have defined the problem, can we read out the problem?" asked Kah Mun, looking at her handiwork. Liza nodded. "Don't forget you read from the left to right."

Mrs. Ganapathy walked round the class looking at the students' work, nodding at some and asking some questions to help others. She listened to some reading the problem to their friends. "This is really good, they are communicating logically," she thought to herself.

"And now, let's look for the win-win solution. One, define the problem, which you have. Two, now focus on the NEEDS boxes and finally, ask whether there is another way to get this need without having to insist on the conflict situation." Liza said and the teacher wrote out the 3-steps in thinking win-win on the board.

"If it is difficult to think of another way to get both sides' NEEDs fulfilled, then you have to start thinking out of the box by looking into your assumptions," continued Liza.

"By asking WHY each side thinks they get their important need by insisting they get what they want? Right, Liza?" asked Nurul.

"Correct!" replied Liza. "And if you see a wrong assumption you will be able to find a solution by providing an alternative way to get your need."

There was so much absorbed discussion that Mrs. Ganapathy was happy. This was one lesson that had all the children busy thinking and communicating. She had a plan now how she could use this TOC Cloud thinking process in her teaching.

IT'S YOUR TURN TO THINK ...

WHAT DO WE GAIN BY CONSTRUCTING THE CLOUD?

- Understand your own position in the conflict.
- Empathy: understanding the other side.
- Understand the emotions involved in the conflict.
- Do not let emotions affect the situation.
- Analyze the problem in a fair way.
- Focus on the core issue of the conflict not the cloudy bit.
- Enable a way to communicate with the other side in a conflict situation.
- Have guidance to come up with Win-Win solutions.

LIST OF DAY-TO-DAY CONFLICTS

"A friend wants to borrow my computer game and I don't want to lend it."

"My best friend wants to copy my project and I want her to do her own work."

"I want to go to a friend's party and my mum doesn't want me to go."

"Eng Joo wants to join our soccer team but we don't want him because he is not a good player."

"I want Ratna to go to the shopping mall with me but she doesn't want to."

TRY THIS!

1. Pick one of the day-to-day conflicts from the list above
2. Write the storyline
3. Construct the cloud to define the problem clearly.
4. Try to find a Win-Win solutions using the steps
5. Use the Cloud diagram below.

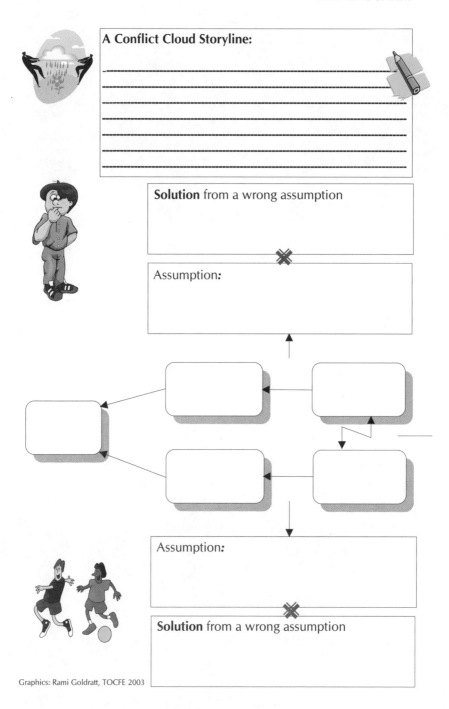

A Conflict Cloud Storyline:

Solution from a wrong assumption

Assumption:

Assumption:

Solution from a wrong assumption

Graphics: Rami Goldratt, TOCFE 2003

45

CHAPTER 9
Meaningful Action:
Understanding Conflict in a Story

 Mrs. Ganapathy was going to teach them a short story. It was a story set in the past, in another country, about a middle class couple who were invited to a high class party. The wife felt it was important to keep her reputation and her social popularity. So she borrowed a beautiful expensive necklace to wear but unfortunately lost it during the party.

The class was listening to the story and allowed to read it up to that point. Standing in front of them Mrs. Ganapathy said, "Well, my dear girls and boys, let's pause here to think about the story using the thinking process we learned before in class, the one called TOC, or Theory of Constraints." Everyone sat up, especially Liza and Nurul.

"I believe that the Cloud can be used to think about making a decision or taking an action in a situation where there is a conflict. You have read the first part of the story. So, tell me can you see any open or concealed conflict?"

A couple of hands immediately shot up.

"I see many actions that may give the woman internal conflicts," said Liza, immediately standing up. "She had to decide whether she should go the high-class party or not to go."

"Yes, or she also has to decide to borrow an expensive necklace or wear something of her own but probably not so beautiful or expensive," said Malliga.

"Very nice, girls," Mrs. Ganapathy said. "Now let me ask before you read the story further. What do you think is the woman's problem now that she has lost the necklace?"

"She has a big problem, teacher," Pradesh said. "Should she tell her friend she has lost the necklace or not tell?"

"I think she could also be thinking about the miserable decision to buy back her friend an expensive necklace with money she doesn't have, meaning she will have to find money for it," Kah Mun said.

"So shall we try and define the woman's problem using the cloud?" asked Mrs. Ganapathy. To Liza's amazement, her teacher started drawing on the blackboard the five boxes connected by arrows, including a zigzag arrow between the boxes on the right. She labelled each side with WANTS and NEEDS and wrote COMMON GOAL beside the fifth box. "Right, let's fill in the diagram. What action shall we look at that has a conflict in it?"

"The woman had to decide between buying a necklace and not tell her friend what happened or tell her friend she had lost the necklace?" suggested Ruzain.

She wrote the two different wants inside the boxes on the right-hand side. "Not tell friend about losing necklace. Tell friend about losing necklace."

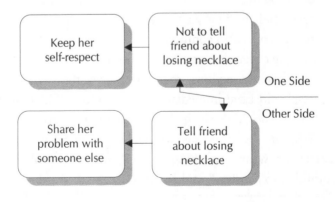

"What is the NEED or important reason for not telling her friend about it?"

"She is a proud woman who needs to keep her self-respect."

"And the other side, what's the NEED or important reason for telling her friend?"

"How about, she needs to share the problem? She can't afford the necklace, so she needs someone to help her tackle the problem."

"So, in order to keep her self-respect, she does not tell her friend she has lost the necklace and in order to share her problem, she has to tell her friend about it."

"Then what will be the desirable situation if she can keep her self-respect as well as share her problem?" Mrs. Ganapathy pointed to the fifth box joined by the two arrows from NEEDs.

"How about she feels relief?"

"No, I think she gets to maintain her self-integrity."

What Mrs. Ganapathy wrote on the blackboard ...

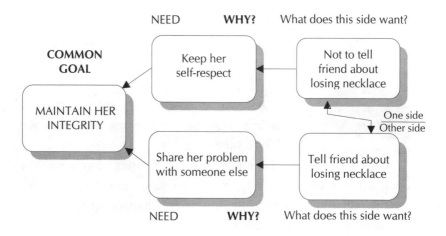

"That's very interesting," declared Mrs. Ganapathy, looking at her Cloud on the board. "We can now read the problem by reading from left to the right."

"Can we help the poor woman solve her problem?" asked Eng Joo.

"Probably, if you use the thinking process," said Mrs. Ganapathy, "but I'd like you to look at this cloud diagram to help you understand the dilemma the character in this story had to go through."

"You're right, teacher," said Nurul. "It makes the story so much clearer than just reading the narrative."

"And I can use the way we read the cloud from the common goal to the opposite WANTS to tell you about the dilemma," said Hadi.

"Good," Mrs. Ganapathy said, "Now I'd like you to identify as many actions that have to be taken by the woman and define her problem."

Guy de Maupausant

"I'd like to try and look at the conflict between the woman and her husband over this matter. I'll do a Cloud on these two sides," Kah Mun said.

"That can be done with the situation of borrowing and not borrowing the necklace, too," Liza suggested.

"Let's put all these different clouds you can come up with on the board. Then as we read the rest of the story, we can use these clouds to discuss what is happening to the main character in the story," their teacher said.

She put several empty boxes in the cloud formation and gave chalks to different students to fill the cloud diagrams on the board.

Liza was really thrilled that they could use the cloud this way with the teacher. She looked round the class, enjoying how her friends were talking so animatedly as they discussed how to define the actions they could find in the story. And there were a lot of cloud 'formations' appearing on the board, too. Her friends were taking notes in their books using cloud diagrams too.

"Right, class. Let's continue with the rest of the story. Take out your book and turn to Guy de Maupausant's story on 'The Necklace' and we will see what actually happened to the poor woman and her dilemma in the original story."

IT'S YOUR TURN TO THINK...

THE CLOUD

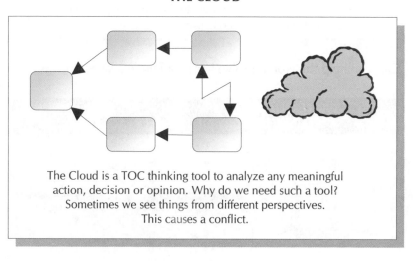

The Cloud is a TOC thinking tool to analyze any meaningful action, decision or opinion. Why do we need such a tool? Sometimes we see things from different perspectives. This causes a conflict.

What Mrs. Ganapathy wrote on the blackboard ...
Read and communicate the problem faced by the woman.

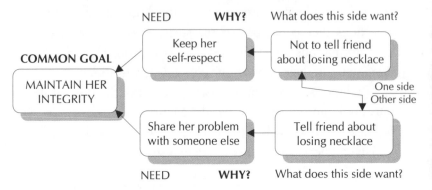

NEED   **WHY?**   What does this side want?

COMMON GOAL

MAINTAIN HER
INTEGRITY

Keep her
self-respect

Not to tell friend
about losing necklace

One side
Other side

Share her problem
with someone else

Tell friend about
losing necklace

NEED   **WHY?**   What does this side want?

COMMUNICATING THE LOGIC IN THE CONFLICT SITUATION

In order to maintain her integrity she must keep her self-respect. In order to keep her self-respect she does not want tot tell her friend about losing the necklace.

On the other hand, in order to maintain her integrity, she needs to share her problem with someone else. In order to share her problem with someone else she wants to tell her friend about losing the necklace

---

Can you help the woman solve her problem in a win-win way?

**WRITE OUT ANOTHER MEANINGFUL ACTION
IN THE STORY OF THE NECKLACE**

Teachers' TIP:
Try using the cloud thinking process on other stories you are reading.
Use this process for differentiated instruction to different ability groups.
Some can define the problem, some work on assumptions and
some come up with win-win solutions

Opposite Courses of Action: Making a Decision

It has been a week since Mrs. Ganapathy used TOC in her class. Some students started practicing the thinking skills process on their own. It was quite easy after their teacher had listed down the steps on how to define a problem using a cloud as well as the three-step process for Thinking Win-Win.

Liza noticed that Hadi seemed very interested and was using the Cloud process to help himself solve his own problems and as everyone knew, Hadi always had plenty of problems.

He came early to school on Monday and immediately caught hold of Liza. "Liza, I used the cloud thinking process to work out a geography topic that had opposite courses of actions."

"So, then what was the result?" asked Liza.

"Well, believe it or not, it works so well I believe I can use this Cloud process to understand the topics or content that show opposite actions or concepts."

"Of course, I believe you," Liza said. "And you know why? It's because the Theory of Constraints is based on systematic and logical thinking so it sorts out the learning and leads to understanding. But I haven't tried it myself. Can you share?"

Hadi rummaged into his school bag and produced a worn-looking notebook. "Remember the topic on the importance of industrialisation and its effects on the environment?"

Liza stared at Hadi's cloud diagram. He had used an amazing way for organising the information. Liza grasped the concept at once just through the diagram.

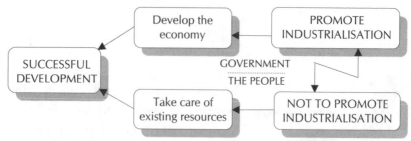

"So you figured the opposing sides in the topic was to have industrialisation or not to industrialised."

"And the two sides will be, the government who would want industrialisation whereas the people living in the area would be against industrialisation," explained Hadi.

"*In order to have successful development, the economy needs to be developed. In order to develop the economy, the government has to promote industrialisation. On the other hand, in order to have successful development, the existing resources have to be taken care of. In order to take care of existing resources, the people living in the area do not want to promote industrialisation.*" Liza was reading from the cloud Hadi had drawn.

"Sounds logical and clear," she added.

"The best part is when I made the link between the opposite actions and the reasons behind each," Hadi explained in an excited voice. "I found that when I asked myself WHY or what is the assumption to say '*In order to develop the economy, the government has to promote industrialisation and when you think BECAUSE ...,*' you'll find that you will be listing all the benefits of industrialisation."

"That helps you understand and remember better, right? Instead of learning all that by memorisation," Liza declared, happy that Hadi had discovered this.

"Right, Liza, and when I go to the other side of the action and think, *in order to take care of existing resources, the people do not want industrialisation* and ask WHY, or what are the assumptions of the people, I realised that they are thinking of the bad effects of industrialisation on the environment."

"Hey, I can see this is going to be a brilliant way of learning some concepts that have opposite actions or decisions." said Liza.

"I am going to show this to our teacher, Mr. Zakaria and see what he says about sorting out the information like this," Hadi said happily. Hadi was seldom associated with a love for academic learning.

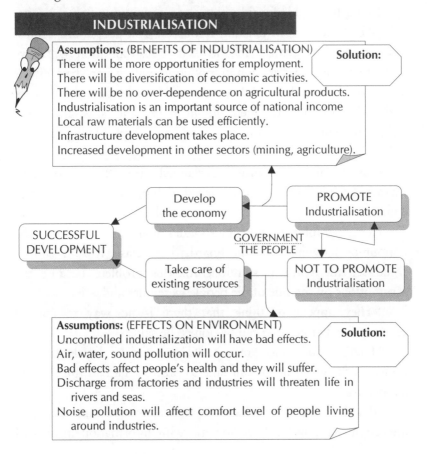

INDUSTRIALISATION

Assumptions: (BENEFITS OF INDUSTRIALISATION) **Solution:**
There will be more opportunities for employment.
There will be diversification of economic activities.
There will be no over-dependence on agricultural products.
Industrialisation is an important source of national income
Local raw materials can be used efficiently.
Infrastructure development takes place.
Increased development in other sectors (mining, agriculture).

Develop the economy

PROMOTE Industrialisation

SUCCESSFUL DEVELOPMENT

GOVERNMENT
THE PEOPLE

Take care of existing resources

NOT TO PROMOTE Industrialisation

Assumptions: (EFFECTS ON ENVIRONMENT) **Solution:**
Uncontrolled industrialization will have bad effects.
Air, water, sound pollution will occur.
Bad effects affect people's health and they will suffer.
Discharge from factories and industries will threaten life in rivers and seas.
Noise pollution will affect comfort level of people living around industries.

"So what are the assumptions made by the government?" asked Liza trying to make out Hadi's scrawl. "Let's see, the government promotes industrialisation because there will be will be more opportunities for employment, diversification of economic activities, no over-dependence on agricultural products. Furthermore, Industrialisation is an important source of national income, local raw materials can be used efficiently, infrastructure development takes place and there is increased development in other sectors such as mining, agriculture."

"You're right, these assumptions work out as benefits for industrialisation."

"Read here," Hadi said pointing to assumptions on the other side. "To take care of existing resources. The people are against industrialisation because uncontrolled industrialisation will have bad effects, air, water, sound pollution will occur, bad effects affects people's health and they will suffer, discharge from factories and industries will threaten life in rivers and seas and noise pollution will affect comfort level of people living around industries."

"Say, Hadi, this is neat!" exclaimed Liza. "Let's show Mr. Zakaria later." Hadi's faced reddened with pleasure. It was a great compliment to be praised on his thinking skills.

The geography teacher liked Hadi's work and Hadi had the honour of showing it on the board to the class. Ruzain said he could see the win-win solutions for this problem because the assumptions on the side of the people were not valid.

"They appear to think that there is no way to control pollution or that nothing can be done," he said.

"That's true," said Pradesh. "There can be legislation and measures the government can take to prevent the bad things from happening."

"Finally," said Mr. Zakaria. "I can see my students taking an interest in learning and feeding me with information instead of waiting to be spoon-fed. Now, how about we use this method to look into the topic of Migration to Cities?"

Mr. Zakaria noticed that for once, no one in class made a disparaging remark when a lesson topic was referred to. Instead, textbooks and notebooks were quickly taken out.

IT'S YOUR TURN TO THINK...

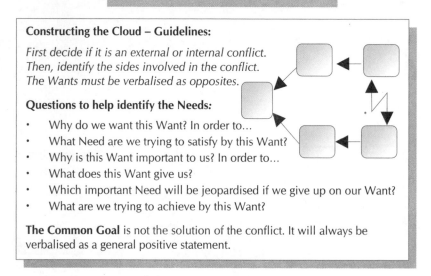

Constructing the Cloud – Guidelines:

First decide if it is an external or internal conflict.
Then, identify the sides involved in the conflict.
The Wants must be verbalised as opposites.

Questions to help identify the Needs:

- Why do we want this Want? In order to...
- What Need are we trying to satisfy by this Want?
- Why is this Want important to us? In order to...
- What does this Want give us?
- Which important Need will be jeopardised if we give up on our Want?
- What are we trying to achieve by this Want?

The Common Goal is not the solution of the conflict. It will always be verbalised as a general positive statement.

Communicating the Logic in the Conflict Situation

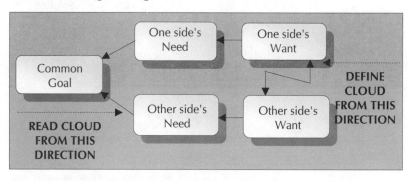

"In order to have ... [Common Goal] ..., I must have ... [my Need] ..."
"In order to have ... [my Need] ..., I must have ... [Want] ..."

SURFACE ASSUMPTIONS AND FIND SOLUTIONS

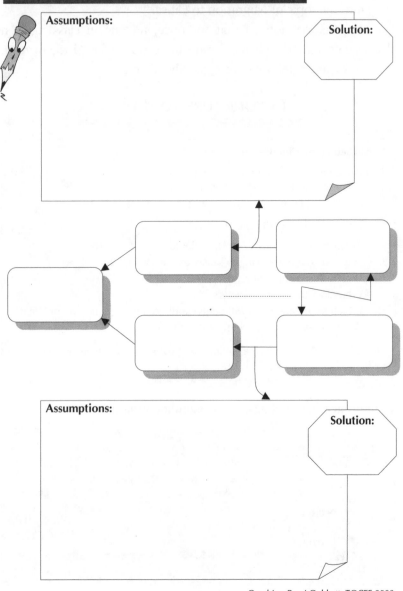

Graphics: Rami Goldratt, TOCFE 2003

CHAPTER 11
Linking Cause and Effect

Liza walked right into a scene one morning. Her friend Kah Mun was standing arms akimbo, glaring at Nurul. Nurul tried to look cool and unperturbed but her fists were clenched at her sides.

"Hey, what's the matter with the two of you?" Liza asked.

"She called me names," said Kah Mun, pointing accusingly at Nurul who just shrugged her shoulders. "She called me Blackie!"

"She's over-reacting," Nurul said. "It was just for fun. She looks so tanned after going to the beach. She can't take a joke."

"Not when I become the centre of your joke!" Kah Mun exclaimed.

Liza looked from one to another. "I think I have to introduce two of you to the next TOC tool I learnt at my holiday workshop."

"What TOC tool?" asked Nurul, distracted for a moment from her anger. "Oh, you mean, Theory of Constraints?"

"I haven't talked to you people yet about the Branch tool and this is just the right time," said Liza, "that is, if two of you can just simmer down and stop glaring at each other." She saw both her friends taking a deep breath as they turned to her.

"Nurul, when you act in a certain way, you must be aware of what happens when you act that way. Tell me, if you call Kah Mun by a name she doesn't like, what happens?"

In LIZA's Notebook

THEN	They stay away from each other

↑

IF **THEN**	Nurul swears back

↑

IF **THEN**	She swears at Nurul

↑

IF **THEN**	Kah Mun gets angry

↑

IF **THEN**	Kah Mun gets offended

↑

IF	Nurul calls Kah Mun "Blackie"

↑

	NEED **To have FUN**

Liza took out her notepad and pencil and wrote "Call her names" at the bottom of the page. She drew an arrow upwards from that.

"If I call Kah Mun names, then she will be offended." Liza wrote that down next and added another arrow upwards.

"Right, then what happens?" asked Liza.

"If she is offended, then she gets angry." Kah Mun nodded on hearing that.

"What will be a reaction?"

"Well, I guess if you hadn't come in, Kah Mun would be swearing at me and then I will swear back at her. Then we might both get angry. If that happens she will stop talking to me or stay away from me." Liza wrote all that down.

"See what I mean?" said Liza, holding up what she had written down for her friends to see. "If we think through how we behave, we will see that there can be negative effects from it. In TOC, this is called a Negative Branch."

"Negative Branch?"

"Yes, it's a chain of events from linking cause and effect starting with someone's behaviour. In this case, Nurul calls Kah Mun 'Blackie'."

"And how does knowing the cause and effect help me?" Nurul asked.

"You said you did it for fun. That was your need that caused the action. So to avoid the eventual effect of losing your friend Kah Mun, you can think of another way of having fun that won't hurt her."

"Oh!"

"You know, Nurul, there are so many ways we can both have fun together," said Kah Mun, putting her arm round her friend's shoulders.

"You're right," Nurul said. "Let's think of some now."

Liza smiled as she saw the two walk off together towards the school canteen.

IT'S YOUR TURN TO THINK ...

THE NEGATIVE BRANCH
The Negative branch is a logical thinking tool that describes through cause-effect relationships how an entry point leads to negative outcomes. The undesirable outcome is directly caused by the person's behaviour.

READING A NEGATIVE BRANCH

If (Cause)....Then (Effect)

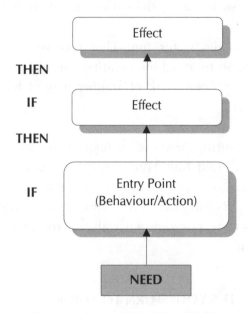

What other ways are there for Nurul to have
FUN with Kah Mun than to call her names?

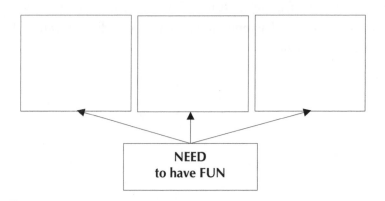

TRY THIS YOURSELF:

1. Now think of an entry point behaviour.
2. Ask "What happens if...?" or "What happens next?"
3. Build a Negative Branch to see what is the final negative implications.
4. Identify your NEED to behave in such a manner.

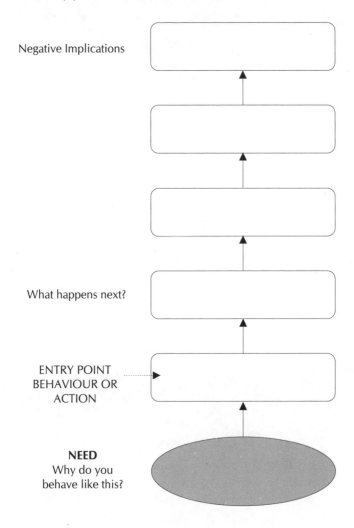

Negative Implications

What happens next?

ENTRY POINT
BEHAVIOUR OR
ACTION

NEED
Why do you
behave like this?

CHAPTER 12
To Change or Not To Change

Mr. Zakaria, the Geography teacher, had left the school for a meeting. The relief teacher had not come in yet. Pradesh, who was tall and thin, sat at the back of the class. He had a group of friends around him.

"What's the matter?" asked Malliga, pointing to the group.

"Pradesh has to report to the discipline teacher today at recess. He was caught by the prefect on duty this morning. Late again for school. Fifth time this month." Nurul shook her head. "He needs your cause and effect Negative Branch thinking skills, Liza. He needs to change his behaviour."

"Pradesh has a problem. But he knows the negative implications of coming late."

"Yes, like he will be punished and he will have demerit points," Kah Mun said, turning to Liza. "So why doesn't he change?"

"Well, there are two other needs that might make him change his behaviour. One, if he thinks he will be rewarded, for example," said Liza. "Or he might change to gain the respect of someone he cares for. So it's not all negative."

"Obviously that's not what makes him tick," Malliga said looking at Pradesh telling his circle of friends how he tried to sneak in through a hole in the fence and got caught by an alert school prefect who was waiting for him. "Look at him bragging about being caught coming late to school many times."

"I think," said Liza, slowly, "I think our friend Pradesh just likes showing disobedience to authority to prove he is in control."

"How can he be in control when he gets punished for it in the end?" asked Kah Mun logically.

"That can mean his need for attention is so strong that he does not think much of the negative outcome of his being late," said Nurul. "We know a lot of people like that. You know, those who want to show themselves as independent and not intimidated by authority."

"Like Pradesh?" asked Malliga thoughtfully, trying to digest the information.

"So how do we help him?" asked Kah Mun.

"He will have to work through his Negative Branch and make himself aware of the long term negative effects from his being late all the time. He can compare that by making a Positive Branch as well. He has to come to that conclusion himself and not be told by someone." Liza made a note in her book.

"I'll get him to sit down and do that so he can think through himself and be in control of his own decision."

"If he practises thinking through often enough, he will definitely end up more responsible," said Nurul, "and that goes for all of us, I guess." She winked at Kah Mun remembering HER own bad behaviour of calling Kah Mun names.

"How do we construct the negative or positive branch?" asked Malliga.

"Like all TOC tools, it's very simple ... here," Liza fished out her notepad again, "you start with the behaviour ...," she drew an arrow upwards, "... and then you ask what happens next, and you keep building upwards using "If ... then ..." like

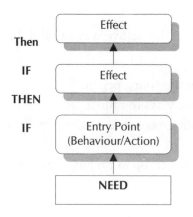

a branch till you reach a negative or positive effect that is meaningful to you."

"And then we ask what is our need behind that bad behaviour and think of another safer positive way of fulfilling the need," said Nurul. "That's easy, isn't it?"

IT'S YOUR TURN TO THINK...

THE LOGIC BRANCH TOOL
The Logic Branch Tool is a logical thinking tool that describes through cause-effect relationships how an entry point leads to negative or positive outcomes directly caused by the person's behaviour.

NEGATIVE AND POSITIVE BRANCHES
We should direct a person to construct a negative branch that starts with the behaviour and ends in significant negative outcomes for him and compare with a positive branch that starts with a change in the behaviour and ends in significant positive outcomes for him.

As long as the original need of the person is more significant than the negative or positive outcomes, he will not change the behaviour. The person thinks that the only way to fulfil the need is by the negative behaviour.

So, what should we do?

We should guide the person to find an alternative way to fulfil the need.

1. Examine the original need of the young person.
2. Think of legitimate alternative ways to fulfil it.
3. Think how to guide the young person in coming up with these ways.
4. Try to guide a member of your group in finding alternative ways.

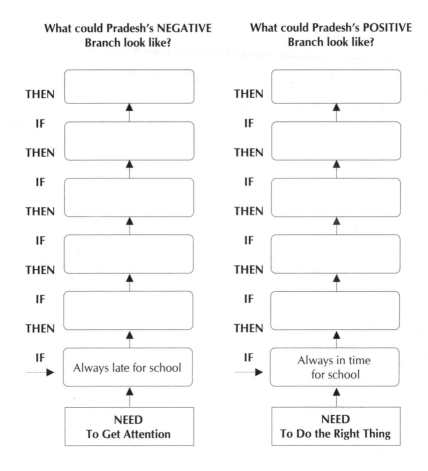

What could Pradesh's NEGATIVE Branch look like?

What could Pradesh's POSITIVE Branch look like?

THEN

IF
THEN

IF
THEN

IF
THEN

IF
THEN

IF — Always late for school

NEED
To Get Attention

THEN

IF
THEN

IF
THEN

IF
THEN

IF
THEN

IF — Always in time for school

NEED
To Do the Right Thing

Pradesh can help himself if he can be aware of negative effects of being late and decide that there are other good, safe ways to get attention.

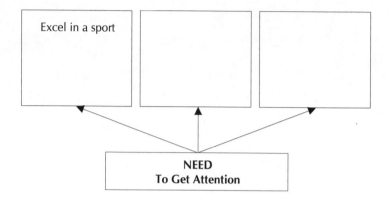

Trimming the Branch

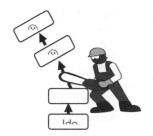

Nurul saw Liza talking to Pradesh at recess. Liza had been trying to get Pradesh on track with his tardiness of coming to school late ever so often.

"So how is it going?" asked Nurul.

Liza gave her a 'thumbs up' gesture.

"I'm not going to pressure him," Liza said. "We discussed his need for attention and other ways of being noticed. He's going to take up hockey seriously because he is quite good at it. Let's see how he does in future, hmm?"

Nurul took hold of Liza's arm. "Liza, I had been thinking of the logic of cause and effect that you used with Kah Mun and Pradesh. It struck me that I could use that for my learning process. You know, how Hadi used the cloud to explain to us about Industrialisation?" She pulled out a piece of paper from her pocket and showed Liza.

"Look at this. I was revising my geography lesson and trying to read up the topic on the implications of population increase. If population increases then overpopulation occurs." Nurul explained.

Liza stared at the scrawls on the paper. "If we want to make the cause and effect process more effective for learning we should add logical supporting information to give deeper insight and understanding," said Liza.

She took out a pen and added to Nurul's diagram.

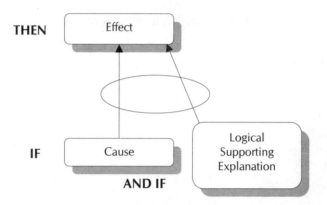

"IF population increases AND IF the rate of economic growth remains the same AND IF the nation's resources are limited THEN overpopulation occurs." Liza added two boxes next to Nurul's. "This will give a clearer explanation on overpopulation because if the other two supporting statements are not there, the next effect may not happen."

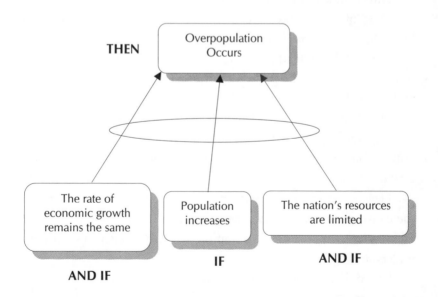

"That's brilliant!" exclaimed Nurul. "Let's look at the rest." The two sat down on a bench and put their heads together to complete the logic branch on the Implications of Population Increase.

On Nurul's Paper ... The Implications of Population Increase

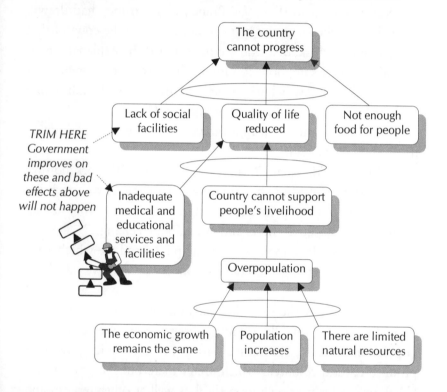

"If overpopulation occurs then the country will not be able to provide for the livelihood of its inhabitants. If the livelihood of the inhabitants cannot be provided for, AND IF medical, education facilities and services are inadequate THEN the quality of life of the people gets worse." Nurul herself added the additional explanations next to her original 'branch'.

"If the quality of life of the people worsens AND IF there is insufficient food AND IF there are inadequate social services THEN the country will not be able to progress!"

Liza scribbled in the remaining conditions and held up the paper. "Hey, Nurul, we have to share this! It's such a neat way of remembering all those facts." She stared hard at the diagram.

Nurul pointed to the Logic Branch diagram they had drawn. "This branch shows all the bad consequences for the country that has a population increase and we have added the explanations or conditions and assumptions to support the effect at each step."

"And you know what?" Liza said turning with a beaming smile at Nurul. "We can trim the branch too!"

Nurul looked at her with a puzzled look. "What's 'Trimming the Branch'?" she asked.

"Oh, I should explain," said Liza. "At my TOC workshop we learnt to think out of the box and ask what changes we can bring about at any suitable point on the Logic Branch and avoid having the rest of the negative effects and bring about a change."

"Hey, let's take a look at the assumptions and see whether we can suggest something the country can do so that we can have progress."

They peered at the scribbled diagram and then Nurul jabbed excitedly at the middle. "How about here? We can't stop population increase, it's difficult to create economic growth or produce natural resources which aren't there but the government CAN improve education and medical as well as other services and facilities and then we will have quality of life!"

"I think we should use this thinking process and discuss this with the geography teacher. I'm sure he'd like this," said Liza.

There was a skip in their steps as they went in search of the geography teacher.

IT'S YOUR TURN TO THINK ...

THE LOGIC BRANCH

If additional information is needed to explain why a cause leads to an effect, chunks of information are explanations or assumptions that can be added in additional boxes to show how one step in the chain leads to the next..

The symbol of a curved line shows the link of information. If we want to TRIM the branch so that it will not lead to the next step, we will have to make the explanation invalid.

ON **WRITING** THE LINK ...   ON **READING** THE LINK ...

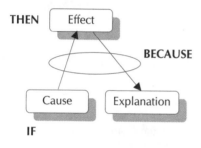

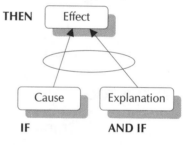

If ... (Cause) ... Then ... (Effect) ...   If ... (Cause) ... And If ...
Because ... (Explanation)   (Explanation) ... Then ... (Effect)

TRY THIS!

Try writing the linking explanation that will cause the effect. Remember you write in the explanation using *'If ... Then ... Because'* but you read it as *'If ... And If ... Then ...'*

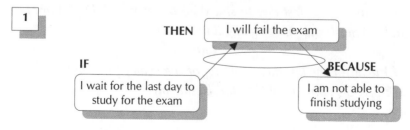

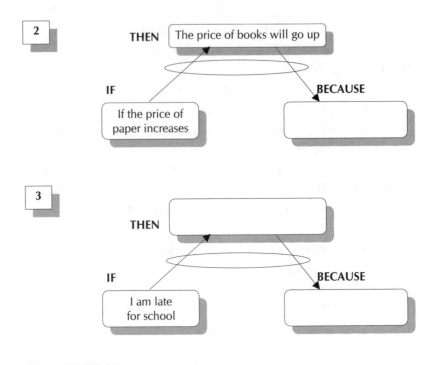

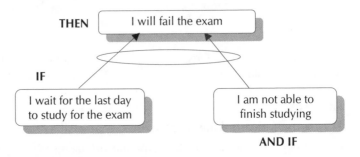

AND IF

Communicating the Cause and Effect

If I wait for the last day to study for the exam AND IF I am not able to finish studying, I will fail the exam.

OR

If I wait for the last day to study for the exam, I will fail the exam BECAUSE I am not able to finish studying.

To make sure that you do not fail the exam you will have to make the explanation "*I am not able to finish studying*" invalid.

What can you do?

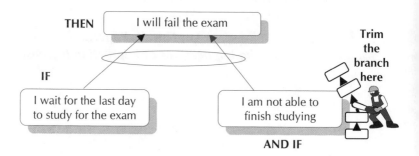

TRIM the branch by suggesting alternatives, for example, "I rely on my master's notes" or even "I understand what my teacher teaches for every lesson" then the outcome will NOT be "I will fail my exams" but will be "I will still pass my exams".

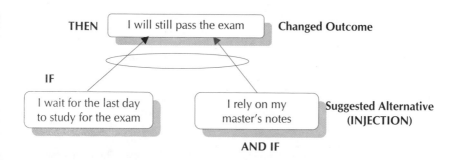

TRIMMING BRANCHES

Can you TRIM any of these branches so that the effect will change by making the explanation invalid and introduce an injection with thinking out of the box?

Then take Nurul's Branch on Population and rewrite it after the TRIMMING, showing the good effects.

Population Increase
(Compare to Branch on page 73)

Complete this BRANCH after trimming it.

On Nurul's Paper...
The Implications of Population Increase

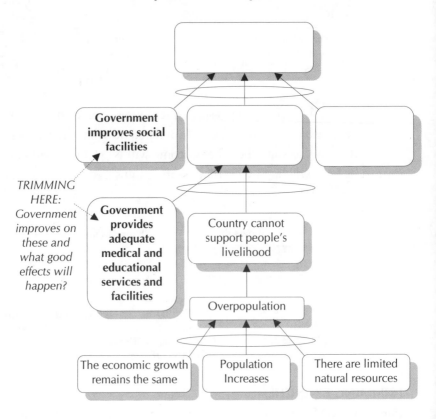

TRIMMING
HERE:
*Government
improves on
these and
what good
effects will
happen?*

Government
improves social
facilities

Government
provides
adequate
medical and
educational
services and
facilities

Country cannot
support people's
livelihood

Overpopulation

The economic growth
remains the same

Population
Increases

There are limited
natural resources

CHAPTER 14
I Have An Idea!

The class monitor called a special meeting after school. Everyone was curious. The Prefects Board had called a meeting during the day and Ruzain had attended it. Everyone knew it was connected to Teachers' Day.

"We have to come up with an idea to do something for Teacher's Day," he said. Everyone turned to their friends and started talking all at once. There was a buzz of excitement.

"I have an idea!" said Eng Joo, finally, loud and clear above the din. Every head turned towards him. His face turned red with the effort of trying to compose his excitement. "Let's do a stage show!"

Immediate reactions followed his suggestion. It sounded like a fish market than a class meeting. "Order, please," Ruzain said, thumping the table with his water-bottle. "Well, what does everyone think?"

Several people tried speaking all at once. Liza's hand shot up and she stood up and cleared her throat. "It sounds like a good idea," she said carefully, "Ruzain, friends, I know of a way of looking at and thinking through a new idea. Do you want to learn how?"

By now, the class had considered Liza as the class sage when it came to thinking processes ever since she had attended her TOC Workshop during the school holidays. "A Theory of Constraints way, I suppose?" Pradesh asked. He had been one of the latest who'd been helped through TOC.

Liza nodded cheerfully. "When evaluating your own ideas or someone else's it is best to first check out what would be the benefits of implementing it."

"Why?" asked Hadi who sat next to Pradesh.

"Well, first, we should be clear about what are the positive outcomes expected from carrying out the idea. You'd want that before anything else,'" said Liza, already at the blackboard with a piece of chalk in hand. "You ask, Ruzain, I'll write them down."

"Right, so what are the benefits from doing a stage show on Teachers' Day? Anyone has any idea?" Hands shot up from all around the group and Ruzain grinned.

"We will have lots of fun planning it!"

"We get to showcase our talents!"

"We show our appreciation of our teachers in a creative way!"

"And we can show our creativity too in our performance!"

"We get to work together to present a good show!"

Ruzain held up his hands. "Okay, okay, looks like we have clear ideas of how it benefits us," he said, looking at Liza who was writing swiftly on the board, "so do we all agree that we should have a stage show on Teachers' Day."

"Yes!" shouted everyone and Eng Joo jumped up and punched the air.

"Right, everyone likes the idea," said Liza. "But we have to be careful when we have a new idea. In TOC, we are taught to look at an idea carefully to make sure we don't encounter negative outcomes when we carry it out and we can also improve on the idea." She put the chalk down and looked at Ruzain, "what do you think, Ruzain? Shall we do just that?"

"Sure, sounds good, like a lot of common sense," Ruzain said. "Just tell us how to go about it!"

IT'S YOUR TURN TO THINK...

Constructive Criticism of a New Idea using a Branch

Often we are approached by someone with an idea which is good but incomplete. This means there are good benefits but there may be negative effects from implementing it.

In order to deal effectively with such an idea we need to encourage the initiative of that person and yet we must make sure the negative outcomes do not happen. We need to get the benefits but not the bad effects from the idea.

The Theory of Constraints identifies the solution as a 3-step process where constructive criticism is provided instead of destructive criticism. How is this done?

The Three-Step Process to Constructive Criticism

1. Understand the idea

When evaluating your own ideas or someone else's it is best to first check and acknowledge what would be the benefits of implementing it. Clearly express the positive outcomes expected from implementing the idea.

2. Understand why the idea should be improved

Improving an idea starts with finding out what can go wrong with it. This can be done by constructing the negative branch in a clear, non-offending manner.

3. Understand how to improve the idea

Find a way to prevent the negative outcomes of implementing the idea. Find an alternative way to get the positive outcomes. One should understand why each step leads to another and find a way to trim the branch.

TRY THIS!

Here are some ideas. Try the first step of understanding the idea by checking the positive outcomes or benefits of the idea.

Example: **IDEA: A Stage Show for Teachers' Day**

1. We will have lots of fun planning it!
2. We get to showcase our talents!
3. We show our appreciation of our teachers in a creative way!
4. And we can show our creativity too in our performance!
5. We get to wok together to present a good show.

I go to the party

_____

_____

_____

_____

I go to the cybercafe after school.

_____

_____

_____

_____

CHAPTER 15
Improving the Idea

 Liza was guiding the class through the process of looking at their idea of having a stage show for Teachers' Day. "We agreed it's a good idea that will benefit us. Now let's look at whether there are possible bad outcomes from it."

Everyone sobered and thought hard. What could go wrong with such a good idea?"

"We need a lot of time to plan and practice," said Malliga.

"Yes we will have to find the time on top of our school work."

"We may quarrel if we argue over who does what job!"

"We've got to find funds for props and costumes."

"We may not do the job well and it will be an embarrassing show!"

Liza put up a hand as she stopped writing on the board. "Hey, folks, you don't have to make it sound so bad. We're not looking at it as something difficult to implement. Let's look at any possible negative outcomes so that we can avoid them and improve on the idea."

She wrote at the bottom of the blackboard: "We have a stage show for Teachers' Day" and she wrote on the top of the board "We have an embarrassing time". Everyone started protesting and Liza held up her hand. She turned to Ruzain, the class monitor.

"It is the worst thing that can happen to this idea, right? So let's see what can happen to make it turn bad. Then we make sure it doesn't happen by trimming the bad outcomes."

"Ahh, trimming the branch," said Ruzain, proud to be able to use a TOC term. "So we should make this negative branch while coming up with the explanations. Let's see, If we have a stage show for Teachers' Day, THEN we will need to plan for the show because staging a show needs strategic planning."

"If we plan for the show THEN we need to give everyone a part because everyone is part of the show. If we do that some may not like what they have been given because not everyone will agree to what they are given. If that happens THEN they will quarrel because everyone likes to assert their rights ... can someone take over from this?"

Liza was busy writing the branch upwards.

Pradesh stood up and took over. "If we quarrel then we will not practise properly because a lot of time is wasted. If we don't then we will put up a poor performance because good shows need a lot of practice." He clasped his forehead jokingly.

"If we give a poor performance then we will have an embarrassing time because the show will be in front of the whole school," finished Nurul. "Now we can see how bad it can be!"

"Well," said Liza. "If we look at the assumptions that explain each effect I believe we can find a faulty assumption. Once we spot that we can invalidate the effect that will result. We can make sure all the bad stuff won't happen. Can anyone help trim the branch so that we can improve the idea?"

"I know," said Hadi, "it's wrong to assume that we won't agree. If we make it a point to be fair allocating duties and not to disagree to what is given to us then the rest of the bad things won't happen!"

"And that is the injection of a sensible step, we have a good improved idea!" said Liza happily. "It's all yours now, Ruzain. Now you plan!"

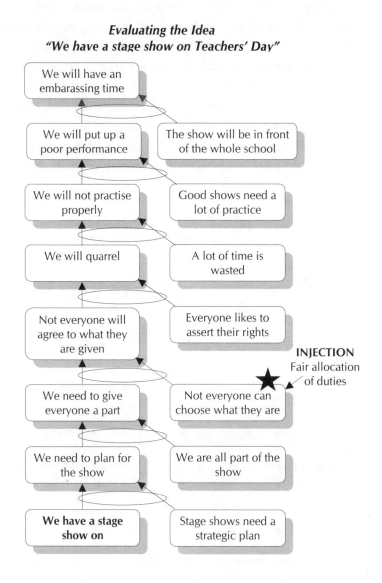

Evaluating the Idea
"We have a stage show on Teachers' Day"

We will have an embarassing time

We will put up a poor performance

The show will be in front of the whole school

We will not practise properly

Good shows need a lot of practice

We will quarrel

A lot of time is wasted

Not everyone will agree to what they are given

Everyone likes to assert their rights

INJECTION
Fair allocation of duties

We need to give everyone a part

Not everyone can choose what they are

We need to plan for the show

We are all part of the show

We have a stage show on

Stage shows need a strategic plan

IT'S YOUR TURN TO THINK...

Improving an Idea using the Negative Branch

How can we improve an idea if we do not know what is wrong with it? To find out what is wrong we use the Negative Branch.

We bring to the surface the reasons for each connection. The arrows leading from one step to another indicates the connection as long as the explanations are valid. If we find any of the explanations invalid we can break the connection and 'Trim The Branch' because the first step will not lead to the next now.

This will result in a greatly improved idea that has good benefits but does not bring bad outcomes on implementation.

We will have a GOOD time

Rewrite the Branch into a positive branch showing an improved idea by putting in the new injection marked.

We need to give everyone a part

We allocate duties fairly to all ★

We need to plan for the show

We are all part of the show

We have a stage show on Teachers' Day

Stage shows need a strategic plan

CHAPTER 16
A Desirable Target

The next few days were full of activity. Everyone had something to suggest for their idea of a stage show on Teachers' Day. Liza watched her friend's antics.

She had volunteered to help make any costumes that were needed. No one needed her yet.

Nurul came by and sat next to Liza. "What a crazy lot of friends we have!" she said.

Liza laughed. She pointed to their friend Malliga. "Look at her, Nurul, sitting there dreaming away."

"What's wrong with her?" asked Nurul.

"Well, Malliga wants to be a great singer, maybe a famous star in future."

"What's wrong with that? It's something she desires for the future."

"Hmm, that's a target she has set for herself. But she has a long way to reach that target. There are many things she can't do yet to become a singer. But she sits there dreaming of being one," explained Liza.

"She's wasting her time?" asked Nurul.

"Exactly!" exclaimed Liza. "Now look at Kah Mun over there. She also aspires to be a good singer and famous star. She's asking people to help her with voice training and she's bravely doing a

87

song item for the show and practising all she can by joining the school choir."

"Malliga has a better voice."

"You're right," Liza said to Nurul, "but you know what's the difference? Kah Mun will be the one who might be successful."

"Why do you say so?"

"When I attended the TOC workshop during the holidays they taught us about Ambitious Targets and how to succeed in achieving them," Liza explained. "There are a few conditions you have to pay attention to."

"And what are these?" asked Nurul.

"First, we have a wish that we want to succeed at something we desire. Then we have to believe that we are able fulfil our wish. And finally we have to work and strive towards succeeding in achieving it."

"That's sensible common sense, isn't it?" Nurul exclaimed. She looked thoughtful for a minute as they looked at Malliga and Kah Mun doing their separate things. "Tell me, Liza, how do we know what we wish is an important target?"

"You mean, as compared to a simple everyday wish that's easy to perform like buying a new book or visiting a zoo?"

"Well, yes, something like that," agreed Nurul.

"Then I'd say that it is a target if achieving it gives you a sense of satisfaction, achievement and a wonderful feeling of accomplishment."

"Would a target be always achievable then?"

"Well, usually we wish for a positive and desirable situation in the future which looks impossible to achieve. That's why many of us just dream about it because we are afraid to work for it and commit ourselves for fear of failure," explained Liza. "Think of a target as the top of a ladder ..."

"That means we have to climb those rungs to reach the top."

"Correct! And each rung seem like an obstacle that blocks you from the top but if you try you can be nearer. Look at Kah Mun singing her heart out in the choir...she's practising and overcoming one rung and going nearer her target, you understand?"

"And how does the Theory of Constraints help us?" asked Nurul.

"It gives you a way to increase your chances of success with a strategic plan!" said Liza. "It's called Dealing with an Ambitious Target."

"Cool," said Nurul. "Now tell me more."

IT'S YOUR TURN TO THINK...

THINKING ABOUT TARGETS

A wish to do something can be just an everyday thing that is easy to perform. Each person should be able to differentiate between this and a target. Achieving a target will give you a feeling of accomplishment, satisfaction and success.

Achieving a target requires:

- a belief in the ability to achieve it
- the commitment to achieve it
- the willingness to devote time and effort towards it
- creating a plan towards it
- carrying out the plan

An AMBITIOUS TARGET will seem very difficult or even impossible to achieve at first glance. That is why people are reluctant to commit to an ambitious target because it seems to have a high rate of failure and people are afraid to fail. There seems to be many obstacles in the way.

What you need to achieve an ambitious target is to have a systematic strategic plan.

An Authentic Personal Target

Try to remember an important target that you wanted to achieve in the past. What was the target?

_____

What was your plan you made to achieve it?

Describe your plan by filling in below:
List the things that prevented you from achieving the target:

_____

In what ways did you try to overcome the obstacles?

_____

Did you have someone who helped you achieve your target? Describe what this person did.

_____

Did you succeed or fail in achieving the target?
Describe your feelings at the end:

_____

Special thanks to Gila Glatter and Shirly Kovalsky for "The Way to Achieving a Target" TOCFE 2000

CHAPTER 17
Dealing with an Ambitious Target

The next week was a bad week for everyone. The class had to cope with a set of monthly tests, sports practices as well as prepare for the stage show. Tempers flared, team members quarrelled, some refused to cooperate. There was a lot of tension.

Liza was seen talking quietly to Ruzain, the class monitor. Ruzain called a special meeting at the end of the day. Mrs. Ganapathy, the English Language teacher, was convinced by Liza into giving them the time.

"Fellow friends," Ruzain said, calling the meeting to order. "We are facing some tough challenges in our project and Liza would like to share with us a way of dealing with our Ambitious Target of 'A successful stage show for Teachers' Day.' She learnt the process during her TOC holiday workshop. I feel we can give it a try." The class clapped in approval and support. Liza felt encouraged.

"Thank you, Ruzain and everyone present for giving me this opportunity," said Liza, going to the front. "We have all agreed on our Ambitious Target that came from Eng Joo's suggestion that we have a stage show for Teachers' Day. It is an exciting target that we all want to succeed in carrying out, right?"

There was a wave of murmurs from the class. "But we are all having disagreements, problems and increasing responsibilities," added Liza. "What we need is a way of dealing with our

Ambitious Target in a systematic way so that we can come out with a strategic plan for success."

"Eh, Liza, you are talking like a big time CEO. This is just a class project," said Pradesh and several of his cronies nodded in agreement.

"When we deal with any Ambitious Target it can be planned by even a preschool kid, Pradesh," Liza said giving him a smile though her voice was firm.

"Okay, okay, no offence meant," said Pradesh, "just making a comment."

"How do we come up with a strategic plan then? We are encountering so many problems." Ruzain looked questioningly at Liza.

"We are feeling pressured because we are afraid that we are going to fail," continued Liza. "So we have to first of all understand and accept that even though we have all agreed on the Ambitious Target, there WILL be obstacles and problems in the way."

She drew a ladder on the board and wrote 'AMBITIOUS TARGET' at the top of the ladder, followed by the class' target.

"These rungs are like the obstacles, see? But if we climb these rungs one by one, they become steps that will help us reach the top. So if we are aware of these obstacles that everyone should try to identify, it can be our strength."

"Meaning, if we know what they are we can think what to do with them?" asked Ruzain. "Hmm, I never thought of it like that before."

"Then we take each obstacle in turn and change it into a positive situation or an action that will overcome the obstacle. It's called a Stepping Stone or an Intermediate Objective."

"Can an obstacle have more than one Intermediate Objective?" asked Hadi.

Liza nodded. "And these steps all bring us nearer to our Target of making a successful stage show for Teachers' Day."

"Is that all for dealing with our target?" asked Kah Mun.

"Not yet. We will then look at all the intermediate objectives and make a Target Tree by arranging what should be done first. Then we look at what alternative actions, who is in charge and when we should achieve each step. Then we have a plan."

"Sounds good and very systematic," said Ruzain. "Shall we start?"

IT'S YOUR TURN TO THINK...

Dealing with an Ambitious Target

An Ambitious Target is a big target that we know is important and worthwhile but is difficult to achieve. Usually we agree that we should achieve it but we have doubts about our chances of doing it.

These are the steps in dealing with an Ambitious Target:

How to Construct a Strategic Plan

STEP 1 Fix the Ambitious Target to be achieved.

STEP 2 Look at the problems and obstacles that are in the way of the target.

STEP 3 Change those obstacles into Stepping Stones or Intermediate Objectives (IOs) or positive statements of the situation.

STEP 4 Use the Stepping Stones or Intermediate Objectives list to decide what should be done first. This step gives you a Target Tree.

STEP 5 Take each Stepping Stones or Intermediate Objectives that has been arranged in order and think of who is responsible and when it should be done.

Now you have a Strategic Plan!

Ensure a commitment to implement the target.

WORDS THAT ARE IMPORTANT

Ambitious Target: A big target that seems difficult to achieve.

Obstacles: A difficulty that is in the way of achieving the target and has to be overcome to achieve the target.

Intermediate Objectives (IOs) or Stepping Stones: A step or action that changes an obstacle into a positive situation.

Target Tree: When the stepping stones are arranged in prerequisite order of what should be done first before the next step, showing a planning process.

TRY THIS!
Change these obstacles into Intermediate Objectives (IOs) or Stepping Stones.

Obstacle: *No one will come to my party*
Positive Stepping Stone: *Find people to come to my party*

Obstacle: *We have too much homework.*
Positive Stepping Stone: --

Obstacle: *We have no transport to the factory.*
Positive Stepping Stone: --

Obstacle: *It is hard to find a time that suits everyone.*
Positive Stepping Stone: --

Obstacle: *We don't have enough money to buy the things needed for the project.*
Positive Stepping Stone: --

CHAPTER 18
Making a Plan

"So our goal is 'A successful stage show for Teachers' Day'," Ruzain said. "Now let's look at all the obstacles."

"Remember, no one can jump from the bottom of a ladder to the top, so everyone's obstacle will be listened to and respected," reminded Liza, "I'll write them on the board. It's okay to list them as they are given."

The next fifteen minutes were pretty lively. Every obstacle they could see was presented and Mrs. Ganapathy, the English Language teacher who had given them the class time, was happy to see the students using English fluently in a real discussion. Liza drew a table with two numbered columns. Soon a list of obstacles appeared on the left column.

"That's it?" asked Liza, looking at the list on the left.

"Looking at this list," commented Kah Mun, "makes it look like the ambitious target is impossible to achieve. There are just too many obstacles!" Many of the others murmured in agreement. Liza held up a hand and Ruzain clapped for attention.

"Hold it. Don't let the list make you feel helpless!" Liza said. "The whole idea is that whenever we have a target to achieve we fail or give up because we let the obstacles overwhelm us."

"Then what are we supposed to do? Celebrate?" asked Hadi, sarcasm in his voice.

"Knowing the obstacles mean we won't feel helpless. Let's change the obstacles to positive steps. Let's see ... We have no theme for the show ... Step: Find a theme! So ... let's go through the list ..." Hands shot up all around the class and very soon, a new list emerged on the right column!

"There!" exclaimed Liza. "Doesn't it look positive now?"

"Right," said Ruzain," now let's see how we can arrange the stepping stones to see what is to be done first. If we add the people involved, a time or date for each step, we will have a plan!"

TARGET: A Successful Stage Show for Teachers' Day

OBSTACLES	STEPPING STONES
1. We have no theme for the show.	1. Find a theme for the show.
2. We have too many items to put in the stage show	2. Have an audition to pick the items to put in the stage show
3. We are unsure whether the quality is good for a stage show.	3. Get the music teacher to assess the quality of the items and show.
4. We have a lot of homework.	4. Approach the teachers to space out our homework.
5. We have sports practices after school.	5. Arrange training and meetings not to clash with sports practices.
6. It's hard to get together at the same time.	6. Make small committees who can meet at different times.
7. We have class tests to prepare for.	7. Arrange training and meetings not to clash with class tests.
8. We have no funds for making stage props.	8. Get ideas to raise funds for making stage props.
9. We need to practice our songs or dances.	9. Decide how much practice we need for our songs or dances.
10. We have no schedule or timetable for practices.	10. Make a schedule or timetable for practices.
11. We have no programme for the show.	11. Make a programme for the show.
12. We have no time to make the stage props.	12. Get parents and other people or those who can't perform to help make the stage props.
13. We have to prepare costumes.	13. Borrow whatever costumes we need and accessorise.
14. We have to coordinate with other programmes in school for Teachers' Day	14. Appoint Ruzain to coordinate with other Teachers' Day programmes in school
15. We have no stage manager.	15. Appoint a stage manager.

IT'S YOUR TURN TO THINK ...

Making a Plan with a Target Tree

When the stepping stones are arranged in order of priority of what should be done first before the next step showing a planning process you get a TARGET TREE which is a thinking tool that helps build a strategic plan to achieve an Ambitious Target.

The steps towards this are:

1. Take the Stepping Stones or Intermediate Objectives that have been suggested as positive steps from obstacles.
2. Arrange these Stepping Stones as what should be done first starting from the bottom. If each Stepping Stones is written on separate papers, it will be easier to arrange the steps.
3. Link arrows to the next step.
4. Some steps are a combination of several stepping stones at the same time. Put these together.
5. The top of the ladder is the target.
6. If each step is given a PERSON in charge and a DATE or TIME to be done you will get an ACTION PLAN.

How to Communicate a Target Tree ...

Reading Top to Bottom:

Ambitious Target

"**Before** *we can have a successful stage show* **we must** *appoint Ruzain to coordinate with other Teachers' day programmes.*"

Graphics: Rami Goldratt, TOCFE 2003

Reading Bottom Up:

> "**We must** *find a theme for the show* **before** *we can have an audition to pick the items to put in the stage show.*"

This is the Target Tree built by Liza's class from their Stepping Stones.

Do you agree with what they decide should be done first?

If not, re-do the Target Tree as you think is best arranged.

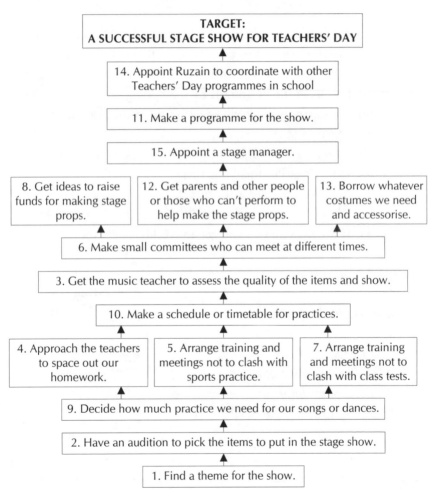

TARGET:
A SUCCESSFUL STAGE SHOW FOR TEACHERS' DAY

↑

14. Appoint Ruzain to coordinate with other Teachers' Day programmes in school

11. Make a programme for the show.

↑

15. Appoint a stage manager.

↑

| 8. Get ideas to raise funds for making stage props. | 12. Get parents and other people or those who can't perform to help make the stage props. | 13. Borrow whatever costumes we need and accessorise. |

↑ ↑ ↑

6. Make small committees who can meet at different times.

↑

3. Get the music teacher to assess the quality of the items and show.

↑

10. Make a schedule or timetable for practices.

↑ ↑ ↑

| 4. Approach the teachers to space out our homework. | 5. Arrange training and meetings not to clash with sports practice. | 7. Arrange training and meetings not to clash with class tests. |

↑ ↑ ↑

9. Decide how much practice we need for our songs or dances.

↑

2. Have an audition to pick the items to put in the stage show.

↑

1. Find a theme for the show.

AN ACTION PLAN:
CHANGING YOUR STRATEGY INTO TACTIC

Liza's class has arranged their Stepping Stones in the order of what should be done first and they have a TARGET TREE which leads them to achieving their target in a systematic way. If they take this order of Stepping Stones and add in more detailed actions, who should do them and when it should be carried out then they will have turned strategy an Action Plan they can use. Try and fill in the rest of the ACTION PLAN.

Target Tree Order	Target Tree Stepping Stones	Significant Actions	Alternative Actions	Who	When
1	Find a theme for the show.	Get class together	Get suggestions	Ruzain	During English class
2	Have an audition to pick the items to put in the stage show	Choose a date	Put up the notice	Kah Mun	After theme is chosen
3	Decide how much practice we need for our songs or dances.	Get a group together	Inform all chosen from audition	Malliga	After audition
4	Approach the teachers to space out our homework.				
5	Arrange training and meetings not to clash with sports practices.				
6	Arrange training and meetings not to clash with class tests.				
7	Make a schedule or timetable for practices.				
8	Get the music teacher to assess the quality of the items and show.				
9	Make small committees who can meet at different times.				
10	Get ideas to raise funds for making stage props.				
11	Get parents and other people or those who can't perform to help make the stage props.				
12	Borrow whatever costumes we need and accessorize.				
13	Appoint a stage manager.				
14	Make a programme for the show.				
15	Appoint Ruzain to coordinate with other Teachers' Day programmes in school				

AN ACTION PLAN:
CHANGING YOUR STRATEGY INTO ACTION

CHAPTER 19
Parameswara's Ambitious Target

The Teachers' Day Stage Show was a great success. Their strategic planning helped them get through the many steps needed to carry out such a great project. Everyone in Liza's class was pleased with themselves.

After their History lesson, Liza noticed Malliga sitting at her desk murmuring to herself and scribbling on a piece of paper.

"Hey, Malliga! What's up? Forgot the *vadai* for recess?" Liza teased. Malliga's eyes were shining with excitement when she looked up.

"Yes?" asked Liza, intrigued by her friend's excitement.

"Liza, I really liked that Ambitious Target thinking process you taught us when we were planning our show. But today when Mrs. Sharifah was teaching us the history lesson on Parameswara in the 15th century ... I think we can use the same thinking process to understand what we are learning!" she started flapping her paper at her friend's nose. "Look at this!"

Intrigued, Liza took the paper and studied it.

"See, I ask myself '*Did Parameswara, the man who founded Malacca, have an ambitious target?*' The answer is 'YES!' Parameswara's goal was to develop Malacca, the place he founded. Right?"

Liza nodded and Malliga went on, referring to her paper. She had put the target on it as: *Parameswara Develops Malacca*. She had drawn two columns, one labelled *OBSTACLES* and the other, *STEPPING STONES*.

"Now when we ask, what were his obstacles in trying to develop Malacca and what do we get? A whole list of them, like his enemies such as the pirates in the Straits, the threat of Siam, the neighbouring country, the strong empire of China, no government structure, no facilities for traders, crime and disorder, boy oh boy, you name it and he has to face them all."

"Then you ask how did he convert those obstacles into stepping stones and what did he do and you get the things he did which we just learnt today in History. You know, what Mrs. Sharifah taught us?"

"Right," said Liza. "He attacked and subdued the pirates to control the Straits of Malacca, sent the Siamese King a tribute in gold to obtain his support, made friends with China by marrying its princess to create an important relationship with a great power, formed a government with Ministers like the *Bendahara* and *Laksamana*, the lot, and introduced laws for crimes, an administrative government process, built trading houses and lodging houses for traders that came from other continents...those were his stepping stones that helped him develop Malacca into a powerful sultanate and centre of trade in his days!"

Target: Parameswara develops Malacca

OBSTACLES	STEPPING STONES
1. Enemies such as the pirates in the Straits	1. Attacked and subdued the pirates to control the Straits of Malacca
2. The threat of Siam, the neighbouring country	2. Sent the Siamese King a tribute in gold to obtain his support
3. The threat of a strong empire like China	3. Made friends with China by marrying its princess to create an important relationship with a great power.
4. No government structure	4. Formed a government with Ministers like the *Bendahara* and *Laksamana*
5. No facilities for traders	5. Built trading houses and lodging houses for traders
6. Crime and disorder	6. Introduced laws for crimes and an administrative government process

"Instead of just reading about this guy Parameswara and his deeds *blah-blah*, putting the historical facts in this way makes me recollect them with understanding. I'm not just memorising. I feel great!"

"And you can show these notes to Mrs. Sharifah and we can have a good time discussing what Parameswara prioritised out of that list of stepping stones."

"You know something?" added Malliga, thoughtfully. "We can even study the target of *The Development of Modern Malaysia* by Tun Dr. Mahathir Mohamad using the same approach."

Liza laughed, putting her arm round her friend's shoulders. "And we can hotly discuss in class too that if one of us in future becomes the Prime Minister of Malaysia what are our obstacles and steps to take to overcome them if we want to develop Malaysia into a world power!"

Malliga stood up. "Let's go share this with Nurul and Kah Mun before we tell Mrs. Sharifah during the next History lesson. Where are they?"

"In the canteen, I suppose," replied Liza. "This is even better than the *vadai* cakes you always bring to share with us."

IT'S YOUR TURN TO THINK...

What kind of content can be taught or learnt using a thinking tool that develops a strategic plan to achieve an ambitious target?

1. When a character wants to achieve something that appears like a significant challenge, e.g. Parameswara develops Malacca.

2. Content that clearly focuses on a target e.g. The Conservation of Rain Forests.

3. Reading the content about an undesirable situation also implies that a target is being jeopardised so developing a

plan to overcome the difficulties can use this thinking process, e.g. Flash Floods in Kuala Lumpur.

4. Concepts can be taught by putting it as a target and building a strategic plan by looking at obstacles and intermediate steps to overcome them, e.g. Pollution, Inflation, Land Utilisation.

TIPS ON CONSTRUCTING A TARGET TREE

1. *Intermediate Objectives* (IO) or *Stepping Stones* can be given as:
   - The opposite of the obstacle
   - An action to overcome that obstacle
2. If you find it difficult to arrange the order of your stepping stones perhaps you need to break that step into smaller steps e.g. Step 1 becomes Step 1a, Step 1b and Step 1c.

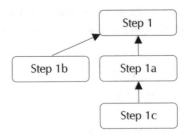

Try this yourself.

1. Pick a subject in school such as Literature, Science, History, Geography, Economics.
2. Choose a topic that has any one of these characteristics:
   - A character wants to achieve something
   - Content that clearly focuses on a target
   - An undesirable situation
   - Concepts that can be put as a target and a strategic plan
3. On a fresh page, write the target on top.

4. List the obstacles faced by the character or the obstacles that prevent the target from success or the problems in the undesirable situation or the obstacles connected to a concept.
5. For each obstacle, change it into a Stepping Stone.

SUBJECT: _____

TOPIC: _____

_____

THE TARGET: _____

_____

Obstacle:	Intermediate Objectives (IOs) *or* Stepping Stones
1.	1.
2.	2.
3.	3.
4.	4.
5.	5.
6.	6.
7.	7.
8.	8.
9.	9.
10.	10.

Constructing a Target Tree

1. Write the Target on top.
2. Take the Stepping Stones.
3. Start from the bottom
4. Arrange them in order of what should be done first, until you reach the target.

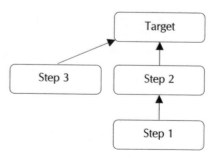

CHAPTER 20
Power of Three

Kah Mun was in a heated discussion with Nurul. They both were in the committee of the school's Geography Society. Liza heard them arguing. She walked over to them and made an inquiring gesture with her chin. "So, you both have a problem, hmm?"

Nurul turned to her. "It's about our new Conservation Project. Kah Mun said that we should use a new approach to run it."

"That's right," said Kah Mun. "A new approach will give the project members the motivation to carry it out. They are bored with the old approach."

Nurul sighed. "Maybe so, Kah Mun. But the old approach is safe and risk free. We don't want to mess things up by trying something new. We have no time to undo any mistakes."

"We all want a successful Conservation Project for the Geography Society," said Malliga who was sitting nearby, "whether we are going to be highly motivated or take a safe boring approach."

"Right," agreed Liza, "we are also making some assumptions right here that in order to be successful we need to be motivated and in order to be motivated we need a new approach because new things will be motivating and on the other hand ..."

"In order to be successful we need to be sure it's safe," Nurul said, "and in order to be safe we use old and tested ways because they have been trouble free all along."

"Ah, a cloud thinking process," said Malliga, dramatically holding up a finger. "So what's the win-win? Or do we have a wrong assumption somewhere?"

"Well, can we be motivated and feel safe?" Nurul asked.

"I'd say, there's a wrong assumption here that we can't make something new as safe as the old," said Kah Mun. "We make sure the new approach is safe."

"But do we know how?" asked Malliga. Liza was smiling as her friends were discussing heatedly.

"Well, we can bring in the Branch thinking process," she suggested, "look at the idea of using the New Approach and see the cause and effect and can we trim the branch to make sure we have no bad effects from the new idea."

"Wow, that's correct," said Kah Mun, "then we can be sure my idea of a new approach has no negative ramifications. Let's try that." Kah Mun already had her pen and paper out and she wrote "Use new approach for Conservation Project" and drew an arrow up.

For the next few minutes, the girls drew the branch from the idea and found where it could go wrong. Kah Mun trimmed the branch herself by suggesting that they put the new idea through an Ambitious Target process so that they would tackle all the obstacles in carrying it out.

"Brilliant, Kah Mun," said Nurul, giving her friend a squeeze in the arm.

"So, my dear friends, do you all realise something?" asked Liza.

"We can now use a new approach for the Conservation Project?" Malliga suggested and everyone laughed.

"Not only that, did you all realise we had used all the 3 TOC thinking processes, the Conflict Cloud, the Branch and the Target Tree together to deal with this issue?" said Liza.

"You're right," marvelled Nurul. "My goodness, the *Power of Three*!"

Her friends thumped her merrily as they knew she was also referring to the popular TV series '*Charmed*' where three sisters who were good witches performed spells as a team of three.

IT'S YOUR TURN TO THINK...

All along we have learnt each TOC thinking process on its own. However when all three are used together it can be a very powerful approach to dealing with a problem.

In this case, using the Cloud can allow us to define and examine the conflict or problem and come out with an injection which is an alternative idea that comes from discovering that an assumption is not valid.

The Branch can be used to check the injection and help show where there is a problem. Trimming the Branch will help ensure an idea does not run into problems.

The corrected idea can now be a Target or goal and surfacing the obstacles will enable us to make sure that these will be taken care of by turning them into stepping stones in the ladder to success.

Mapping the action steps from the first important step to the goal will create a TARGET TREE which will ensure that the strategic implementation can take place. Finally the problem will be solved.

Power of Three Thinking Processes

1. Try this. Fill in the cloud on Kah Mun and Nurul's problem in the story:

The Conservation Project:
School Geography Club

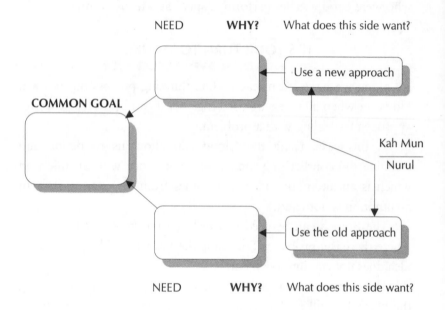

A Cloud Thinking Process
THE SCHOOL CONSERVATION PROJECT

Any wrong assumptions?
Solution from a wrong assumption?

Communicate the problem defined
"In order to ... (Common Goal) ...,
   Nurul has to ... (Nurul's NEED) ... ,
   in order to ... (Nurul's NEED) ...,
   she ... (Nurul's WANT) ..."

Assumption:
Using Old Approach won't mess up
   the project
Old Approach is trouble free

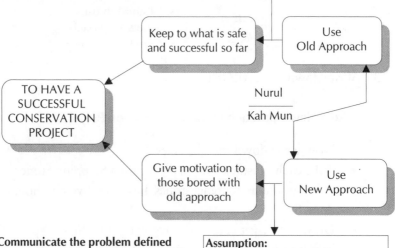

Keep to what is safe
and successful so far

Use
Old Approach

TO HAVE A
SUCCESSFUL
CONSERVATION
PROJECT

Nurul
―――――
Kah Mun

Give motivation to
those bored with
old approach

Use
New Approach

Communicate the problem defined
"In order to ... (Common Goal) ..., Kah
   Mun has to ... (Kah Mun's NEED) ... ,
   in order to ... (Kah Mun's NEED) ...,
   she ... (Kah Mun's WANT) ..."

Assumption:
In order to be successful we need to
   be motivated

Any wrong assumptions?
Solution from a wrong assumption?

113

2. Write down the idea 'Use a New Approach' as the beginning of your Branch. Now complete the branch using 'IF ... THEN ...' to see the possible effects from it. Try to trim the branch to achieve a positive outcome.

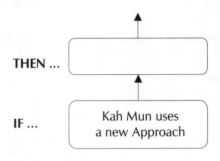

3. Write down the TARGET:

'Use a New Approach in the Conservation Project'

- Now write down the obstacles
- Take each Obstacle and make it into a Stepping Stone
- Arrange these stepping stones based on which should be done first
- Draw a Target Tree by arranging the first step at the bottom and the Target is right at the top of the Tree

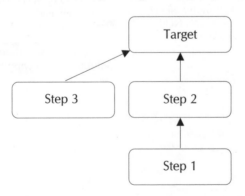

CHAPTER 21
Empowering Ourselves

The holidays were only a week away. Everyone in school was already in a holiday mood as the mid-year exams were finished. Ruzain was at his best as class monitor, making sure everyone was happy and being firm when anyone stepped over the line.

"Well, Liza, what are you going to do this time?" asked Nurul.

"What do you mean?" asked a puzzled Liza.

"The last school holidays you went to a TOC Workshop, remember?"

"Oh I see," Liza smiled at her friends. "There's another TOC Workshop for this school holidays." Her friends closed in on her.

"Tell us more. Are you going again?"

"No, not as a participant. I'm going as a cucumber!"

"Cucumber!" Everyone shouted all at once, looking at her, incredulously.

Liza giggled. "That's the name they call assistants who help at TOC Workshops," she explained. "I've been invited as a cucumber."

"But why?" asked Eng Joo, scratching his head of spiky hair.

"Cucumbers walk around the room. We keep everyone cool and collected," replied Liza. "Honestly, it's true!"

"Do you think we should attend a TOC Workshop like you did?"

"Why not?" Liza asked. "It will help you to improve yourselves as I have with myself. I am not worried when I am faced with challenges or problems because TOC gave me ways to deal with them."

"If I think about it, for problem-solving I would like the Cloud process in my pocket," said Ruzain. Everyone looked at him.

"Why do you say that?"

"Well, at the core of almost any problem or decision that we face is always the dilemma of doing one thing or the other. It's useful to understand a problem and knowing it is not choosing between what we want that is in conflict but knowing what we need."

"Goodness, you sound ... um ... so profound," said Malliga admiringly.

"Well, I like the Branch thinking process," said Hadi. "I am always asked to explain myself and the Branch is great for communication and clarification and allows me to predict what can happen and trimming allows me to change the future, so to speak. Very powerful, you know."

"I would say it's a great one to keep you safe, seeing you are always getting into trouble," Pradesh told him. They all laughed because that was just like Hadi to get himself into trouble all the time.

"Personally I like the Ambitious Target tree," chirped in Kah Mun. "It allows me to turn undesirable obstacles into desirable steps."

"I agree," Malliga said. "It's so natural for people to point out why things can't be done. And the people who raise the obstacles best understand how to deal with them. In the end it's a great process to get cooperation."

Liza stood up, looking at her friends. "I am SO impressed by all of you. I think by learning TOC thinking tools we are empowering ourselves with the ability to become responsible people who can make good decisions. Don't you all agree?"

The Process of On-Going Improvement

THE PROCESS OF CHANGE

TOC Thinking tools help in the process of on-going improvement. There are 3 questions to ask to be able to achieve a major strategic improvement from what you start out with.

What to Change?

This is a statement of the problem. If we want to improve, we require a change. Improvement is a valid reason for change. This is where you define the problem that could be based on wrong assumptions or erroneous perceptions.

To What to Change?

This is a statement of the solution. If we understand the first question of what to change, we will understand that this second question refers to the replacement of the problem situation for something better. For this we need out of the box thinking to get improvement.

How to Cause the Change?

This refers to the implementation of the change for improvement. A lot of times this stage meets with obstacles from people. Using TOC Thinking Tools help to enable the obstacles to be removed so that change can occur.

The Process of On-Going Improvement

Once we have caused the change we have to go back to the whole process starting again from What to Change. This is known as POOGI or the Process of On-going Improvement.

CHANGE TO LIFELONG SKILLS

What to Change

Children need to solve problems themselves, make responsible decisions, make plans and communicate their ideas.

To What to Change

We teach them to do these themselves instead of waiting for adults to do these for them.

How to Cause the Change

Using the Cloud, The Branch and The Ambitious Target Thinking Processes

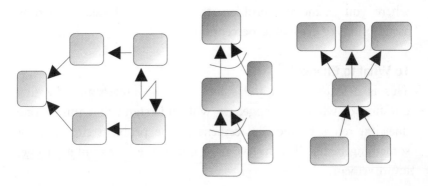

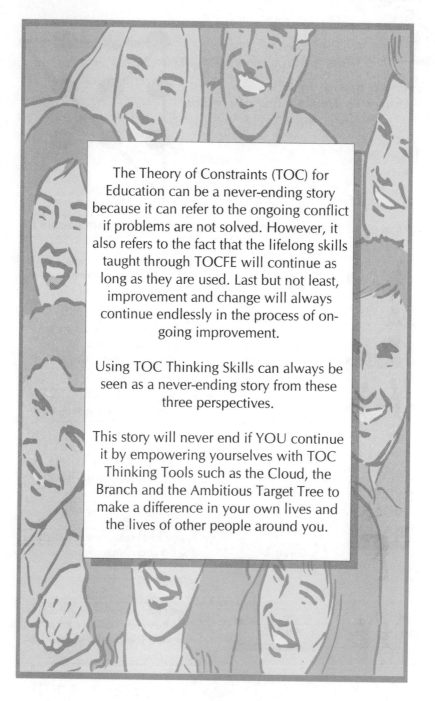

The Theory of Constraints (TOC) for Education can be a never-ending story because it can refer to the ongoing conflict if problems are not solved. However, it also refers to the fact that the lifelong skills taught through TOCFE will continue as long as they are used. Last but not least, improvement and change will always continue endlessly in the process of on-going improvement.

Using TOC Thinking Skills can always be seen as a never-ending story from these three perspectives.

This story will never end if YOU continue it by empowering yourselves with TOC Thinking Tools such as the Cloud, the Branch and the Ambitious Target Tree to make a difference in your own lives and the lives of other people around you.

Answer to page 35
Answer To Thinking Out of The Box

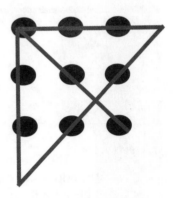

Answers to page 26

Common Ways of Dealing with Conflict

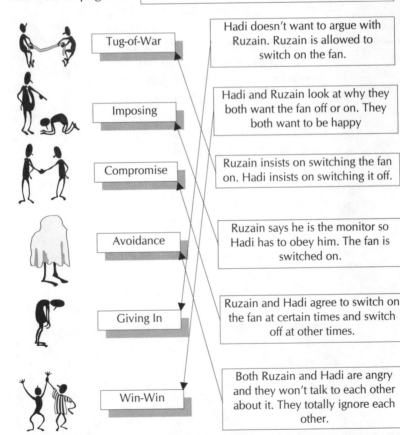

Tug-of-War

Imposing

Compromise

Avoidance

Giving In

Win-Win

Hadi doesn't want to argue with Ruzain. Ruzain is allowed to switch on the fan.

Hadi and Ruzain look at why they both want the fan off or on. They both want to be happy

Ruzain insists on switching the fan on. Hadi insists on switching it off.

Ruzain says he is the monitor so Hadi has to obey him. The fan is switched on.

Ruzain and Hadi agree to switch on the fan at certain times and switch off at other times.

Both Ruzain and Hadi are angry and they won't talk to each other about it. They totally ignore each other.

Index